D0066127

Heart-Cry for Revival

Heart-Cry for Revival

Expository Sermons on Revival

STEPHEN F. OLFORD

Oh that thou wouldest rend the heavens, that thou wouldest come down, that the mountains might flow down at thy presence.

ISAIAH 64:1

FLEMING H. REVELL COMPANY

COPYRIGHT © MCMLXII BY FLEMING H. REVELL COMPANY

Westwood, New Jersey
All rights reserved

Library of Congress Catalog Card Number: 62-10738

Printed in the United States of America

1.1

Acknowledgment is given for:

Lines from a hymn by R. Hudson Pope, quoted by permission from *C.S.S.M. Choruses No. 2.*

Portions of the *Revival Prayer Fellowship News Sheet,* quoted by permission.

"Screwtape Proposes a Toast," © 1959 by Helen Joy Lewis. Reprinted from *The World's Last Night* by C. S. Lewis by permission of Harcourt, Brace & World, Inc.

Permission to quote from an article by the Reverend Duncan Campbell which appeared in *The Christian Herald,* January 10, 1953.

Quotation from R. V. G. Tasker, *Tyndale New Testament Commentaries,* published by Tyndale Press and William B. Eerdmans, reprinted by permission.

Permission to use portions of an open letter written by Dr. Frederick A. Tatford and published in the *Harvester Magazine.*

Part of an editorial by Dr. A. W. Tozer for *The Alliance Witness,* January 25, 1956, by permission.

Christianity Today for permission to quote portions of an article written by Dr. C. Gregg Singer in the June 19, 1961 issue.

Dedicated to

all those who share with me a

Heart-Cry for Revival

INTRODUCTION

I COUNT IT A MOST HAPPY PRIVILEGE TO WRITE THE INTRODUCtion to this book, the author of which has been one of my closest friends for more than two decades. Indeed he and I have been intimately associated with one another in the Lord's work, and have been drawn into a very precious fellowship of prayer and service through these many years. We have not only prayed together but wept together, laughed together, preached together and stood side by side on many occasions to make known the claims of our risen Lord, and to offer Him to the people.

In a recent time of such fellowship, Mr. Olford and I shared some of the convictions that find expression in this book which, I believe, go right to the heart of the most urgent need of our day, namely, Holy Spirit revival in the church. I am so thankful to find the burden of my dear friend's heart expressed so clearly in print, as I have heard him express it intimately to the Lord and publicly in the name of the Lord to the people. It is a heart-cry which I can truly say I share without any reservations whatsoever, and only pray that I may yet live to see that burden become a reality through my own ministry, as well as in the ministry of hundreds of others in the Lord's work.

It is my deep conviction that we are in grave danger of allowing ourselves to be sidetracked into launching an anti-Communist crusade in the conviction that all the sin is on the other side of the fence. What is urgently needed is a deep humiliation of heart before God and a repentance and brokenness of spirit in His presence as is expressed in the cry of Ezra: "O Lord God of Israel, thou art righteous: for we remain yet escaped, as it is this day: behold, we are before thee in our trespasses; for we cannot stand before thee because of this" (Ezra 9:15).

Surely God does not burden the hearts of His people, as He has done the author of this book, to mock us. Surely He will yet rend the heavens and come down, that the mountains might flow down at His presence (Isaiah 64:1).

I am confident that this book will have a great ministry to the hearts of all who read it, and none who do so can ever be the same again.

ALAN REDPATH
Moody Church
Chicago

PREFACE

THE FOLLOWING EXPOSITORY SERMONS ON REVIVAL, IN THEIR present form, were first preached from the pulpit of the Calvary Baptist Church, New York City. Later they were delivered at the "Keswick Convention" in Jamaica, W.I., and Prairie Bible Institute in Alberta, Canada. The one message they spell out is a "Heart-Cry for Revival"—born out of a study of God's Word, and the desperate need of the church of Christ, today. They make no claim whatsoever to scholarship or literary excellence. As a matter of fact, the sermons, in the main, are typescripts from tape recordings of my preaching. This will account for their sermonic style and personalized application.

I am deeply indebted to my dear friend and colleague in the ministry, Dr. Alan Redpath, for his gracious Introduction, and also to those concerned for granting me kind permission to quote extensively from the life of *Joseph W. Kemp* and C. S. Lewis' book *The World's Last Night;* and last, but not least, to those who have labored lovingly to help prepare the manuscript. Other sources of information are gratefully acknowledged elsewhere in the book.

Without doubt, the greatest encouragement to publish this material came, in the first instance, from the president of *The Sunday School Times,* Mr. C. Stacey Woods, and also the editor, Mr. James W. Reapsome. It was they who originally received the sermons for use in the columns of the above-mentioned magazine, and saw the further possibilities for this ministry.

So I send forth this little book with a sincere prayer that the burden which God has given me for a spiritual awakening in our day may become a Heart-Cry for Revival on the part of all who read these pages.

STEPHEN F. OLFORD
Minister, Calvary Baptist Church
New York City

CONTENTS

Heart-Cry
for Revival

1

The "WHAT" of Revival

To understand the burden of this little book, I feel it is necessary that my readers should be introduced to the frame of reference in which I write. Without the definition of terms, and explanation of aims, I might well be misunderstood. So by way of introduction, I want to state briefly what I consider to be the nature of, the need for, and the nearness of revival.

I THE NATURE OF REVIVAL

The term "revival" is one which is grossly misunderstood. In many quarters today it is employed to describe evangelistic meetings. Then, there are others who understand by this word the restoration of backsliders. Now while the salvation of sinners and the restoration of backsliders are both by-products of revival, these spiritual experiences cannot be said to define revival.

In seeking to find an answer to the question "What is revival?" I am taking the liberty of quoting freely from several authorities who have written on the subject. William B. Sprague says: "Wherever you see religion rising up from a state of comparative depression to a tone of increased vigor and strength; wherever you see professing Christians becoming more faithful to their obligations, and behold the strength of the Church increased by fresh accessions of piety from the world; there is a state of things which you need not hesitate to denominate a revival of religion."

Charles G. Finney defines revival as: ". . . nothing else than a new beginning of obedience to God. Just as in the case of a converted sinner, the first step is a deep repentance, a breaking down of heart, a getting down into the dust before God, with deep humility, and a forsaking of sin."

G. J. Morgan puts it this way: "It is reviving humanity, strictly speaking, to the sense of God—through the indwelling of the Holy Spirit—to reanimate the life of the believer, not to the unregenerate, as they are 'dead in trespasses and sins.' There can be no reviving, as there was no life to revive. But whenever Christians are revived, there will always be the conversion of men. It has a twofold meaning, implying the revival of spiritual life and vigor among Christians and the conversion of sinners. It is God manifesting Himself through human life, His redeeming power bursting forth in fruits of righteousness and holiness, in the constitution of His Church, the reproduction of spiritual life, a fresh incarnation of the gladness, the rapture of the gospel of the Galilean fields, of the anguished cry of Pentecost rising into a doxology of redeeming love."

Arthur Wallis, in his book entitled *In the Day of Thy Power*, writes: "The meaning of any word is determined by its usage. For a definition of revival we must therefore appeal to the people of God of bygone years, who have used the word with consistency of meaning down the centuries, until it came to be used in a lesser and more limited sense in modern times. Numerous writings on the subject that have been preserved to us will confirm that revival is divine intervention in the normal course of spiritual things. It is God revealing Himself to man in awful holiness and irresistible power. It is such a manifest working of God that human personalities are overshadowed, and human programs abandoned. It is man retiring into the background because God has taken the field. It is the Lord making bare His holy arm, and working in extraordinary power on saint and sinner."

J. Edwin Orr, who has written so extensively on revival, and whose notable work on the *Second Evangelical Awakening in Britain* should be read by all, sums up our theme in this fashion: "The best definition of revival is the phrase, '. . . Times of refreshing . . . from the presence of the Lord.' "

Joseph W. Kemp, in a presidential address to the Baptist Union of New Zealand, declared: "Revival, strictly speaking, means the reanimating of that which is already living but in a state of declension. It has to do principally with the Church as a whole and Christians as individuals. Evangelism, in our usage of the word, as well as in its derivative sense, refers primarily to the proclamation of the gospel to the unsaved. To make evangelism a synonym of revivalism is untrue to the teaching of the New Testament. The Church is responsible for evangelism and not for revival. We are summoned to evangelism; for revival we are cast upon the sovereign grace of God."

From these and many other definitions that could be quoted, we gather that revival is that strange and sovereign work of God in which He visits His own people, restoring, reanimating and releasing them into the fullness of His blessing. Such a divine intervention will issue in evangelism though, in the first instance, it is a work of God in the church and amongst individual believers. Once we understand the nature of heaven-sent revival, we shall be able to think, pray and speak intelligently of such ". . . times of refreshing . . . from the presence of the Lord" (Acts 3:19).

II THE NEED FOR REVIVAL

There has never been a time in the history of the church when God's people have not had a heart-cry for revival. Even in the midst of appalling moral darkness and spiritual declension, there have always been the faithful ones whose heart-cry has been:

> Oh that thou wouldest rend the heavens, that thou wouldest come down, that the mountains might flow down at thy presence,
> As when the melting fire burneth, the fire causeth the waters to boil, to make thy name known to thine adversaries, that the nations may tremble at thy presence!
> When thou didst terrible things which we looked not for, thou

camest down, the mountains flowed down at thy presence. *Isaiah 64:1-3*

Speaking for our time, however, I see no hope whatsoever outside of the coming again of our Lord Jesus Christ or a mighty spiritual awakening. This conviction was expressed in unmistakable language sometime ago by outstanding leaders of the Christian Brethren in an open letter published in the *Harvester* magazine. Ponder carefully this appeal:

It is doubtful whether, in the history of the world, there has previously been a period of difficulty so complex in character and so widespread in effect as that through which we are at present passing. A feeling of uncertainty and instability prevails in every circle, and the future seems to hold no sure promise of either peace or prosperity. It was never more true that "upon the earth" there is "distress of nations, with perplexity; . . . men's hearts failing them for fear, and for looking after those things which are coming on the earth."

In the midst of change and unreliability, spiritual values alone remain immutable, and there never was a greater need for the reminder of their reality, security, and stability. Yet the Church, which should be proclaiming the glorious news, seems totally inadequate to meet the need. Generally speaking, the lives of Christians do not differ, to any great extent, from the lives of other folk around them. They share the same fears, express the same doubts, feel the same uncertainty, show the same disconcertion. The peace of God and the joy of Christ are little in evidence. The dynamic power of the Holy Spirit is not appropriated.

Unparalleled opportunities present themselves, but there seems a moral and spiritual inadequacy to respond to their challenge.

If there is to be a revival of spiritual life and power, it must originate with the individual believer, and there is a great need for a personal searching of heart and exercise of soul in this matter. The sin, which is spoiling the life of the Christian, must be judged, and put away. The selfishness, which is robbing Christ of the love and devotion which are His due, must be confessed and removed. The ambitions and desires, which are hindering the work of God, must be uprooted and thrown on the refuse heap. A renewal of blessing is dependent upon the restoration of communion and the reconsecration of heart and life.

Many of God's people are longing for a reawakening of the Church and for a revival of the work of God, and not a few are praying that the very conditions of the present day may lead to a reassessment of values and a fresh stirring of love for the Lord.

A renewal of evangelistic fervor and zeal might even yet result in an amazing harvest of souls, and we appeal to all Christians to unite in daily personal prayer, not only for a solution to the pressing practical problems of the present day, but for a definite spiritual revival.

If I understand the contemporary scene at all, then it is my conviction that we are up against four major trends in the life of *the evangelical church,* which make the need for revival urgent and desperate.

The first is what I am electing to call *Biblical objectivism,* in genuinely conservative evangelical circles. Our main problem is not liberalism, nor even neo-orthodoxy; that which threatens us is a subtle, objective approach to the Bible, to theology, and to preaching in general, which is unrelated to holy living. We are all busy with our dispensational charts, attractive book analyses, and our Bible memorization programs—all excellent in and of themselves—but, nonetheless, strangely remote from practical living. Audiences sit and listen week by week to this kind of teaching without any evidence of transformed characters and Spirit-anointed witnessing. The preaching itself mysteriously lacks the authority of heaven and the relevancy to our times which brings about deep conviction, repentance, faith, and obedience. Young and old return from so-called Bible conferences without any evidence of having met with God. True, there are exceptions to this general state of affairs, but any burdened Christian knows that this picture is not overdrawn. O that God would teach us that it is just as important to be spiritual as to be sound in our approach to the Bible, just as vital to be obedient as to be orthodox, and that the purpose of revelation is nothing less than transformation of human lives!

The second menace is that of *overt antinomianism.* When God's Word is not related to life in terms of *absolute* commands and demands, then morals and standards cease to exist.

Thus the philosophy of the "double standard" has been introduced into our modern way of living; and, in this sense, the world has set the standards for the church.

Some while ago, one of the leading secular magazines in the United States of America, commenting on the work of Dr. Alfred C. Kinsey, stated "that the most significant aspect of Dr. Kinsey's survey in this country is the wide gap between sex behavior and the law, as now constituted. America's morals and sex laws go back to the Hebrew Talmud, with a Jehovah God of vengeance towering over the miscreant with a stern 'Thou shalt not.' Such sex taboos were incorporated into English laws at the time of the Puritans, and from there were lifted bodily into the American laws. The Kinsey survey shows, however, that 85 per cent of the people of the United States habitually violate the law—and could be prosecuted if their sexual activities were known!"

The article goes on to say that it has been revealed that by the age of fifteen, 92 per cent of American males have had sex experience. The feminine population is twenty-nine years old before a similar percentage is reached. The report also shows that about one third to one half of all married men are unfaithful to their wives at one time or another. It might be argued that while this is true in the world, this is not necessarily the situation in the church. The sad fact is evident to all who have eyes to see, however, that the spirit of antinomianism is invading all sections of evangelical life.

One of our outstanding Christian magazines published the findings of a questionnaire that was used among young people who were from predominantly Christian homes and evangelical churches. It was stated that most of these young people professed to be saved, and many of them did not attend movies and dances. Yet it was discovered that in the area of morals there was a complete breakdown: "78 per cent of these boys, between the ages of fifteen and twenty, reported having had illicit sexual relations with girls. The majority of these indicated that such behavior occurred *after* their conversion."

My own experience amongst young people and, alas, older

folk as well, confirms these findings. The tragedy is that so many confess to ignorance of moral standards or, otherwise, take pride in the fact that they are keeping up to date with modern trends. God have mercy on us!

The third menace which confronts us is what I term *democracy gone awry*. For some time I have kept this to myself until I could analyze the situation accurately and prayerfully. Then I came across one pastor after another who expressed the same views and, still later, I was brought into touch with writings which have corroborated my growing conviction. Our founding fathers never intended that democracy should be an excuse for the contempt of authority and the refusal to recognize God-ordained leadership. No one has put this more clearly than Dr. C. Gregg Singer, Professor of History at Catawba College, Salisbury, North Carolina. He says:

> The American dream is vanishing in the midst of the terrifying realities and visible signs of decadence in our contemporary society. But it would be false to infer that the crisis of the present is the cause of its disappearance as a vital factor in American life.
>
> The dream itself was built on an unstable foundation, for it did not emanate fully from that biblical outlook which guided colonial life. There was a colonial dream for the New World which the colonists brought with them as a part of their heritage from the Reformation, and which motivated them as they forged a new civilization out of the wilderness. It was their desire to found a society which would be based on biblical principles.
>
> But this colonial dream of the early settlers with its biblical orientation gave way before the onslaughts of the Enlightenment and the rise of the democratic philosophy of the American Revolution. Out of the War of Independence there arose a new American dream whose chief architects were Thomas Jefferson and Thomas Paine. This American dream was not derived from biblical principles, but reflected the naturalism and humanism of deism and the emerging democratic philosophy. Thus it contained the elements making for its own dissolution. For it was based on an optimistic view concerning the nature of man and a belief in the perfectibility of the race. Not only was it unbiblical, but at the same time it encouraged a type of political, social, and economic action which

could only hasten the destruction of any society which accepted these false views.

At first glance the democratic insistence on the equality of all men may seem to be little more than a political and social expression of the biblical doctrine of the priesthood of the believer. But such is far from the case. Underlying the democratic philosophy is the humanistic insistence on man's sovereignty and inherent goodness.

The crisis which has overtaken not only the United States but Western Europe is but the unfolding of the catastrophic nature of the Enlightenment of which the American dream soon became the offspring. The awesome conflicts of our era are not the cause of the dilemma, but rather are they the outward manifestation of the deadly cancer which is in fact eating away the very soul of the West.

If that is from the pen of an American writer, let us see what C. S. Lewis has to say on the subject. In his book *The World's Last Night* he has a chapter entitled "Screwtape Proposes a Toast." The scene is in Hell at the annual dinner of the Tempters' Training College for Young Devils. The principal, Dr. Slubgob, has just proposed the health of the guests. Screwtape, a very experienced Devil, who is the guest of honor, rises to reply. In the address that follows (which every Christian should read) the Devil says this:

Democracy is the word with which you must lead them by the nose. The good work which our philological experts have already done in the corruption of human language makes it unnecessary to warn you that they should never be allowed to give this word a clear and definable meaning. They won't. It will never occur to them that *Democracy* is properly the name of a political system, even a system of voting, and that this has only the most remote and tenuous connection with what you are trying to sell them. Nor of course must they ever be allowed to raise Aristotle's question: whether "democratic behavior" means the behavior that democracies like or the behavior that will preserve a democracy. For if they did, it could hardly fail to occur to them that these need not be the same.

You are to use the word purely as an incantation; if you like, purely for its selling power. It is a name they venerate. And of course it is connected with the political ideal that men should be equally treated. You then make a stealthy transition in their minds from this political ideal to a factual belief that all men *are* equal. Especially the man you are working on. As a result you can use the word *Democracy* to sanction in his thought the most degrading (and also the least enjoyable) of all human feelings. You can get him to practice, not only without shame but with a positive glow of self-approval, conduct which, if undefended by the magic word, would be universally derided.

The feeling I mean is of course that which prompts a man to say *I'm as good as you*.

The first and most obvious advantage is that you thus induce him to enthrone at the center of his life a good, solid resounding lie. I don't mean merely that his statement is false in fact, that he is no more equal to everyone he meets in kindness, honesty, and good sense than in height or waist measurement. I mean that he does not believe it himself. No man who says *I'm as good as you* believes it. He would not say it if he did. The St. Bernard never says it to the toy dog, nor the scholar to the dunce, nor the employable to the bum, nor the pretty woman to the plain. The claim to equality, outside the strictly political field, is made only by those who feel themselves to be in some way inferior. What it expresses is precisely the itching, smarting, writhing awareness of an inferiority which the patient refuses to accept.

And therefore resents. Yes, and therefore resents every kind of superiority in others; denigrates it; wishes its annihilation. Presently he suspects every mere difference of being a claim to superiority. No one must be different from himself in voice, clothes, manners, recreations, choice of food. "Here is someone who speaks English rather more clearly and euphoniously than I—it must be a vile, upstage, lah-di-dah affectation. Here's a fellow who says he doesn't like hot dogs—thinks himself too good for them no doubt. Here's a man who hasn't turned on the jukebox—he's one of those goddam highbrows and is doing it to show off. If they were honest-to-God all right Joes they'd be like me. They've no business to be different. It's undemocratic."

Now this useful phenomenon is in itself by no means new. Under the name of Envy it has been known to the humans for thousands of years. But hitherto they always regarded it as the most odious, and also the most comical, of vices. Those who were aware of feeling it felt it with shame; those who were not gave it no quarter in others. The delightful novelty of the present situation is that you can sanction it—make it respectable and even laudable—by the incantatory use of the word *democratic.*

Under the influence of this incantation those who are in any or every way inferior can labor more wholeheartedly and successfully than ever before to pull down everyone else to their own level. But that is not all. Under the same influence, those who come, or could come, nearer to a full humanity, actually draw back from it for fear of being undemocratic. I am credibly informed that young humans now sometimes suppress an incipient taste for classical music or good literature because it might prevent their Being Like Folks; that people who would really wish to be—and are offered the Grace which would enable them to be—honest, chaste, or temperate, refuse it. To accept might make them Different, might offend against the Way of Life, take them out of Togetherness, impair their Integration with the Group. They might (horror of horrors!) become individuals.

All is summed up in the prayer which a young female human is said to have uttered recently: "O God, make me a normal twentieth-century girl!" Thanks to our labors, this will mean increasingly, "Make me a minx, a moron, and a parasite."

Meanwhile, as a delightful by-product, the few (fewer every day) who will not be made Normal and Regular and Like Folks and Integrated, increasingly tend to become in reality the prigs and cranks which the rabble would in any case have believed them to be. For suspicion often creates what it suspects. ("Since, whatever I do, the neighbors are going to think me a witch, or a Communist agent, I might as well be hanged for a sheep as a lamb and become one in reality.") As a result we now have an intelligentsia which, though very small, is very useful to the cause of Hell.

But that is a mere by-product. What I want to fix your attention on is the vast, over-all movement towards the discrediting, and finally the elimination, of every kind of human excellence—moral, cultural, social, or intellectual. And is it not pretty to notice how *Democracy* (in the incantatory sense) is now doing for us the work that was once done by the most ancient Dictatorships, and by the same methods? You remember how one of the Greek Dictators (they called them "tyrants" then) sent an envoy to another Dictator to ask his advice about the principles of government. The second Dictator led the envoy into a field of grain, and there he snicked off with his cane the top of every stalk that rose an inch or so above the general level. The moral was plain. Allow no pre-eminence among your subjects. Let no man live who is wiser, or better, or more famous, or even handsomer than the mass. Cut them all down to a level; all slaves, all ciphers, all nobodies. All equals. Thus Tyrants could practice, in a sense, "democracy." But now "democracy" can do the same work without any other tyranny than her own. No one need now go through the field with a cane. The little stalks will now of themselves bite the tops off the big ones. The big ones are beginning to bite off their own in their desire to Be Like Stalks.

This *democracy gone awry* is rampant in our free churches. You can see it and sense it in action when you preach on the Lordship of Christ, on the authority of the Word, and on the imperatives of holiness. You try it and observe it for yourself!

The fourth enemy of true evangelicalism is *religious materialism.* That sounds like a paradox, and in one sense it is, but I can describe it in no other way. It is the unspoken belief in the hearts of leaders and laymen that God is not needed in most of our Christian work. All that is required is the almighty dollar, high-pressure salesmanship, efficient organization, personality parade, and modern gadgets—and revival will come, souls will be saved, and the church will be built up. Of course prayer will be offered and God's blessing invoked, but as far as trusting God in naked faith, as the early disciples did, that never seems to matter now. Thank God there are some choice and rare exceptions to this, both in individual lives and in local churches. But on the whole, there is so little Spirit-begotten and energized prayer, so little utter dependence upon God, so little authoritative preaching; instead there is so much of high-pressure appeals for money, for decisions and for uninstructed membership in our church life. These and many other disturbing features on the contemporary scene make me long and cry out for revival. Some people call me a pessimist, but I claim I am not a pessimist, nor an optimist, but a realist. That is what I have seen and experienced and I do not believe that there is any solution other than a mighty spiritual awakening. What is more, outside of healthy evangelism, I do not see that we are justified in expecting anything less than the showers of the "latter rain" ere the Lord Jesus returns to harvest the precious fruit of the earth.

III THE NEARNESS OF REVIVAL

One of the encouraging evidences that God is moving across the face of the earth in stirring up His people to seek revival is the little prayer cells that are emerging everywhere. For some years now I have been associated with the Revival Prayer Fellowship, which was commenced some years ago at St. Paul's Church, Portman Square, London, England. The leading spirits behind this fellowship are the Reverend Prebendary Colin Kerr and Mr. George S. Ingram. Every month they send out a *News Sheet* which is filled with reports from these prayer cells, representing every part of the world. I am accustomed to reading such news flashes as these:

INDIA: Over 50 people in this city are now meeting in small groups for prayer. . . . Now over 550 prayer cells have come into being all over India, and the Lord has given us over 2000 pledged members in the All India Prayer Fellowship. . . . Kindly keep praying with us that He will send the mighty downpour of the Holy Spirit. [By the Secretary of the All India Prayer Fellowship for Revival.]

PAKISTAN: God's Spirit is at work in many places in West Pakistan, and we pray that these many little fires may soon merge into one mighty flame of revival!

NEPAL: Just recently Nepali Christians themselves started meeting on the first Friday night of each month, praying with you for revival in this and all lands.

ARCTIC REGIONS: Our people here in the Arctic are working and praying hard for revival. This is part of the life of the church of the north country. I was at a meeting of two groups of Eskimos who have a prayer meeting once a week, praying for revival, and I was conscious of the power that seemed to emanate from those two meetings.

EASTERN EUROPE: This is to testify that, even behind the Iron Curtain, there are believers who have heard about the Night of Prayer, and enjoy to take part in it at the same time. They are only a few but faithful ones. It is just wonderful to taste this heavenly fellowship of His followers all around the world.

FREE CHINA: The . . . courage that comes with reading your news letter makes our hearts rejoice. I have just laid down yours of March, 1961 and thank God for it. The newspaper leaves an utterly different impression—just as different as darkness from light. I finished the one and prayed, "Lord have mercy on us." And I finished your word and rejoiced and prayed, "Lord, let us be among those who are prepared for the revival which the godly elder, quoted in that News Sheet, in Wales says You are surely bringing." And I believe he is right: the Lord is about to send Revival. [By a missionary.]

Many other examples of what is taking place in these prayer groups could be cited, but these will suffice to illustrate the heart-hunger for revival.

Every now and again Christian magazines will report on a revival which has visited a church or a town. One such event took place recently in Wainwright, Alaska. Up until this divine visitation, most of the town's 250 inhabitants were associated with its two churches, Presbyterian and Assemblies of God—in name only. Few had ever experienced a definite conversion. Today virtually all of Wainwright has turned to Jesus Christ. Following special meetings, God moved in and results were spontaneous. People righted wrongs, renewed friendships that had been severed for years. In one meeting in the Presbyterian Church, all but two of the seventy-five present dedicated their lives to God. Miles away, out on the tundra, a young man with his sled and dog team suddenly became so aware of the presence of the Lord that he returned to the village a changed man. The report goes on to say that many have stopped using tobacco, others enrolled in Bible study courses, despite language barriers. Formerly the village had two movie projectors. Today, so many people attend church instead that only one remains, and it is in operation only three nights a week!

Another story which has come to hand is that of an unusual outpouring of the Holy Spirit in the churches near Farmerstown, Ohio, under the ministry of Joshua Daniel of south India. Entire congregations were overcome by a sense of spiritual need, and wept openly, unashamed, like little children. Public confession followed, and members who had been at variance for years made things right. During the period of this local revival, Daniel gave himself to fasting and prayer, and at night he preached the Word with great power. "I am very often in a spirit of mourning over the state of American churches," Daniel said. "America has a leading part in the Christian world, and sends out many missionaries, but they can never rise above the spiritual level of their home church. Unless you have true revival here, we in other lands are going to be hit hard if you keep sending out missionaries to us. Your shallowness will reflect on us."

Some of us still remember a spiritual awakening which visited the Hebrides in 1949. God's servant used in this gracious moving of the Holy Spirit was the Reverend Duncan Campbell. In recounting the story of God's dealing with His people in the Hebrides, Mr. Campbell stated:

I personally believe in the sovereignty of God in the affairs of men, but I do not believe in any concept of service that eliminates man's responsibility. Here are men and women who believe in a covenant-keeping God; who believe that the God to whom they pray could not fail to fulfil His covenanted engagements; but they also believe that they too had to do something about it. God was the God of Revival, but they were the instruments, the agents through which revival was possible. I heard one of the Elders of the church praying: "Lord, You must do it, for we cannot; but we want to tell You now that we are here before You as empty vessels for You to fill." Such was their confidence and conviction as they lingered in the presence of God, month after month, three nights a week, meeting together in a barn at ten P.M., and remaining there before God until four and five o'clock in the morning. Yes, they believed that revival was coming, but they also knew that a price had to be paid.

They waited. The months passed, and nothing happened, until one morning—at about two o'clock, I believe—one young man, known very well to the Lewis converts, took up his Bible and read from Psalm 24. "Who shall stand in His holy place? He that hath . . . a pure heart; who hath not lifted up his soul unto vanity, nor sworn deceitfully. He shall receive the blessing from the Lord." Not OUR blessing, but THE blessing.

The young man closed the Bible and looking at his companions on their knees before God, he cried: "Brethren, it is just so much humbug to be waiting thus night after night, month after month, if we ourselves are not right with God. I must ask myself—'Is my heart pure? Are my hands clean?' " And at that moment, a moment that will live in the memory of Lewis, something happened. God swept into that prayer group and at that wonderful moment seven Elders discovered what they evidently had not discovered before, that revival must be related to Holiness. "Is my heart pure? Are my hands clean?" Yes, at that moment, they found themselves in the searching power of the presence of God and discovered things about themselves they had never suspected. But the Blood of Calvary heals and cleanses.

As I have already said, God swept into the meeting and seven men were now lying prostrate before Him. Do not come to me at the end of this meeting and ask me to explain the physical manifestation of this, because I cannot explain, but these men moved at that moment from the sphere of the natural and found themselves lifted to the realm of the supernatural. These men knew that Revival had come.

These manifestations of God's willingness to revive His people have been witnessed in our day. Surely this should encourage us to believe in even greater things in our own personal lives and local churches. Indeed, to me, these sounds ". . . of a going in the tops of the mulberry trees . . ." (II Samuel 5:24) are a clear indication of the nearness of revival—if only we were ready in this day of His power.

The real issue, then, is how to be ready in the day of His power. To help us in our thinking and praying, and also to condition our hearts for the chapters that follow, I want to quote an editorial from the pen of the beloved Dr. A. W. Tozer, editor of *The Alliance Witness*, and, in his own right, a prophet of righteousness and revival:

I have previously shown that any Christian who desires to may at any time experience a radical spiritual renascence, and this altogether independent of the attitude of his fellow Christians.

The important question now is, How? Well, here are some suggestions which anyone can follow and which, I am convinced, will result in a wonderfully improved Christian life.

1. Get thoroughly dissatisfied with yourself. Complacency is the deadly enemy of spiritual progress. The contented soul is the stagnant soul. When speaking of earthly goods Paul could say, "I have learned . . . to be content"; but when referring to his spiritual life he testified, "I press toward the mark." So stir up the gift of God that is in thee.

2. Set your face like a flint toward a sweeping transformation of your life. Timid experimenters are tagged for failure before they start. We must throw our whole soul into our desire for God. "The kingdom of heaven suffereth violence, and the violent take it by force."

3. Put yourself in the way of the blessing. It is a mistake to look for grace to visit us as a kind of benign magic, or to expect God's help to come as a windfall apart from conditions known and met. There are plainly marked paths which lead straight to the green pastures; let us walk in them. To desire revival, for instance, and at the same time to neglect prayer and devotion is to wish one way and walk another.

4. Do a thorough job of repenting. Do not hurry to get it over with. Hasty repentance means shallow spiritual experience and lack of certainty in the whole life. Let godly sorrow do her healing work. Until we allow the consciousness of sin to wound us we will never develop a fear of evil. It is our wretched habit of tolerating sin that keeps us in our half-dead condition.

5. Make restitution wherever possible. If you owe a debt, pay it, or at least have a frank understanding with your creditor about your intentions to pay, so your honesty will be above question. If you have quarreled with anyone, go as far as you can in an effort to achieve reconciliation. As fully as possible make the crooked things straight.

6. Bring your life into accord with the Sermon on the Mount and such other New Testament Scriptures as are designed to instruct us in the way of righteousness. An honest man with an open Bible and a pad and pencil is sure to find out what is wrong with him very quickly. I recommend that the self-examination be made on our knees, rising to obey God's commandments as they are revealed to us from the Word. There is nothing romantic or colorful about this plain downright way of dealing with ourselves, but it gets the work done. Isaac's workmen did not look like heroic figures as they digged in the valley, but they got the wells open, and that was what they had set out to do.

7. Be serious-minded. You can well afford to see fewer comedy shows on TV. Unless you break away from the funny boys, every spiritual impression will continue to be lost to your heart, and that right in your own living room. The people of the world used to go to the movies to escape serious thinking about God and religion. You would not join them there, but you now enjoy spiritual communion with them in your own home. The devil's ideals, moral standards and mental attitudes are being accepted by you without your knowing it. And you wonder why you can make no progress in your Christian life. Your interior climate is not favorable to the growth of spiritual graces. There must be a radical change in your habits or there will not be any permanent improvement in your interior life.

8. Deliberately narrow your interests. The Jack-of-all-trades is the master of none. The Christian life requires that we be specialists. Too many projects use up time and energy without bringing us nearer to God. If you will narrow your interests God will enlarge your heart. "Jesus only" seems to the unconverted man to be the motto of death, but a great company of happy men and women can testify that it became to them a way into a world infinitely wider and richer than anything they had ever known before. Christ is the essence of all wisdom, beauty and virtue. To know Him in growing intimacy is to increase in appreciation of all things good and beautiful. The mansions of the heart will become larger when their doors are thrown open to Christ and closed against the world and sin. Try it.

9. Begin to witness. Find something to do for God and your fellow men. Refuse to rust out. Make yourself available to your pastor and do anything you are asked to do. Do not insist upon a place of leadership. Learn to obey. Take the low place until such time as God sees fit to set you in a higher one. Back your new intentions with your money and your gifts, such as they are.

10. Have faith in God. Begin to expect. Look up toward the throne where your Advocate sits at the right hand of God. All heaven is on your side. God will not disappoint you.

If you will follow these suggestions you will most surely experience revival in your own heart. And who can tell how far it may spread? God knows how desperately the church needs a spiritual resurrection. And it can only come through the revived individual.

I will praise thee with my whole heart: before the gods will I sing praise unto thee.
I will worship toward thy holy temple, and praise thy name for thy lovingkindness and for thy truth: for thou hast magnified thy word above all thy name.
In the day when I cried thou answeredst me, and strengthenedst me with strength in my soul.
All the kings of the earth shall praise thee, O Lord, when they hear the words of thy mouth.
Yea, they shall sing in the ways of the Lord: for great is the glory of the Lord.
Though the Lord be high, yet hath he respect unto the lowly: but the proud he knoweth afar off.
Though I walk in the midst of trouble, thou wilt revive me: thou shalt stretch forth thine hand against the wrath of mine enemies, and thy right hand shall save me.
The Lord will perfect that which concerneth me: thy mercy, O Lord, endureth for ever: forsake not the works of thine own hands.

PSALM 138

2

The "WHO" of Revival

THIS PSALM IS ONE OF A GROUP OF EIGHT ATTRIBUTED TO DAVID. We are not very sure of the history of its writing. Some believe that it is one of the many psalms that were rediscovered in later years. One thing is evident, however: it is a glorious paean of praise to Jehovah in a time of great deliverance. David had been fainting and God had heard his prayer and revived him. Listen to his words: "In the day when I cried thou answeredst me, and strengthenedst me with strength in my soul. . . . Though I walk in the midst of trouble, thou wilt *revive me:* thou shalt stretch forth thine hand against the wrath of mine enemies, and thy right hand shall save me. The Lord will perfect that which concerneth me: thy mercy, O Lord, endureth for ever: forsake not the works of thine own hands" (vss. 3, 7 and 8).

Of recent times the word "revival" has come to mean something quite different from the original thought implied in this term. So many use it to denote evangelistic meetings and general gospel work. But this is not the accurate biblical or historical connotation. When we use revival, we mean the sovereign act of God, in which He restores His own backsliding people to repentance, faith and obedience.

The question often arises as to why God withholds revival if it is wholly His prerogative to send it. When given serious thought, the answer is plain. God can never fill capacities that are not equal or open to His revival fullness. We must remember that while it is God who alone visits men in revival, He must be allowed room in which to work. This brings us abruptly to "the *who* of revival." The answer is threefold. God revives those who are prepared to:

I CONFESS SPIRITUAL FAILURE IN THEIR LIVES

"In the day when I cried thou answeredst me, and strengthenedst me with strength in my soul. . . . Though I walk in the midst of trouble, thou wilt revive me" (vss. 3, 7a). Revival presupposes failure. It is only those who admit failure and fainting whom God truly revives. In the physical realm, when a man faints and is weak, he needs reviving. In the New Testament we find certain words which are the spiritual expression of a fainting man. The first one is *Prayerlessness*. Jesus said: ". . . men ought always to pray, and not to faint" (Luke 18:1). If a man is not praying, he is fainting. The word "to faint" here is "to cave in" or "to break down." Does that describe your prayer life? Is that why you need revival? It is my profound conviction that prayerlessness is the outstanding sin in the church of Jesus Christ today. The least popular and the worst attended gathering so often is the prayer meeting. Since the church is made up of individuals, the question comes back to you and me: What about prayerlessness in your life, in my life? How we need to cry with David, "Thou wilt revive me."

Dr. Sidlow Baxter has vividly and pungently stated the need for intercessory prayer in the following words:

> We need a revival of intercessory prayer among God's own people. We do not pray enough. Besides intensifying their private prayer life, Christians should band themselves into cottage prayer groups to lay hold upon God for revival in our own land and in every land. Our most pressing need at this moment is to ask God to give more mighty prayer to all who can have at heart the speedy evangelization of every unreached soul—prayer that is strong, prevailing, believing, God-moving, hell-defeating, devil-routing, sinner-saving, believer-sanctifying, Christ-exalting, worker-producing and money-finding!—prayer that takes all we are and have, to offer it to God, as it took all that Jesus had, on Calvary, to give us the right to pray.

But where in all the world are we going to get prayer that will do that?—the kind that Daniel offered, which shook the Babylonian Empire from end to end, bringing Almighty God into His rightful preeminence; the kind that Nehemiah offered, which set rulers running after him with men, money, and materials, to help rebuild the walls of ruined Jerusalem. It was God Himself Who inspired the prayer of Nehemiah, the prayer that made Jerusalem a new city. He drove His servant to his knees by the burden of a great concern for ruined Jerusalem. This seems to be the way God works. And will God give this kind of prayer today? Yes, through the Holy Spirit, God can give us the hurricane kind of prayers that make things move when nothing else can make them move.

We must get God's prayer—prayer with extraordinary consequences! Prayers which are merely our own are futile and get us nowhere. The devil fears nothing that man makes—not even his prayers! He only begins to feel alarm when a soul begins to offer before God the prayer that is Spirit-inspired, and which was born in the very heart of God Himself. It is prayer shot through with the very blood and passion of the Son of God, filled with the power and persistence of the Holy Ghost, loaded with a burdening sense of the church's plight, and the world's appalling need, that sets the wheels of Revival in motion!

God save us from trying to turn these wheels by our own efforts! It cannot be done. Let us beg God now for this kind of praying—prayer straight from God, to straighten out every tangle and to meet every need. When we offer His prayer, as put into our spirits, there will be no such thing as unanswered prayer. Every prayer will be as almighty as God, because His nature will be in them. The difficulties we face at the present time will vanish, and we shall not speak as if God were bankrupt!

God will then be seen in our lives. His power will flow through us in flood-tides of blessings to others. Miracles will happen in every sphere that we touch. Every need will be met; and the devil will be defeated. May this heaven-born flame be lighted afresh in the hearts of the regenerate throughout the world.

But fainting in the spiritual life is also an evidence of *Fearfulness.* You will remember how the writer to the Hebrews challenges this sin of fearfulness when he writes: ". . . consider him that endured such contradiction of sinners against himself, lest ye be wearied and faint in your minds. Ye have not yet resisted unto blood, striving against sin" (Hebrews 12:3, 4). The word "faint" this time means "to relax," or "to let out rope." How many Christians are relaxing instead of fighting against sin; letting out rope with evil instead of coming to grips with it and slaying it in the name of the Lord. In the Book of Jeremiah God says to us, ". . . cursed be he that keepeth back his sword from blood" (Jeremiah 48:10). Can you honestly say, "As God is my record, I am *not* afraid of holiness; I am *not* fearful of going through with God, cost me what it will; I am *not* going to hesitate because of being thought spiritual"?

Fainting not only suggests prayerlessness and fearfulness, but also *Barrenness*. ". . . let us not be weary in well doing," says Paul, "for in due season we shall reap, if we faint not" (Galatians 6:9). This term "faint" also carries the thought of "relaxing" or "letting out rope"; and the Apostle points out that to faint or relax in this sense is to be barren, to lose the joy of harvest. ". . . we shall reap, if we faint not." Is the need of revival in your life a confession that you are barren in life and service? Let us then face up to it and be honest in our confession of failure. Let us pray and mean the words—"Lord revive me for I am prayerless, fearful and barren."

In the next place I want you to see that God is waiting to revive men and women who are prepared to:

II PROFESS PRACTICAL FAITH IN THEIR LIVES

". . . thou wilt revive me . . ." (vs. 7a). James reminds us that ". . . faith without works is dead" (James 2:20). A working faith is one which believes in the ability of God to do anything that is in the divine purpose and for the divine glory. In this context it is faith in *a God of Personal Revival*. ". . . thou wilt revive *me* . . ." (vs. 7a). All through the Bible we have instances of the divine and human encounter. When Abraham reached the point in his life when he was prepared to give his all, God said to him, ". . . because thou hast done this thing. . . . in blessing I will bless thee . . ." (Genesis 22:16, 17). Later we read of Jacob who, having been broken by the heavenly wrestler, cried out, ". . . I will not let thee go, except thou bless me" (Genesis 32:26). Then you remember the impassioned prayer of Jabez, "Oh that thou wouldest bless me indeed . . ." (I Chronicles 4:10).

So often we dodge the real issue of revival by praying for it generally, not recognizing that before God can bless others He wants to bless us personally. Mrs. Elizabeth Codner sensed this *personal* need when she wrote her hymn, "Even Me." This was in 1860, when revival was taking place in Ulster and Wales, and she longed that the blessing might visit her and spread through England. Weigh the words carefully:

Lord! I hear of showers of blessing
Thou art scattering full and free—
Showers the thirsty soul refreshing;
Let some drops now fall on me,
Even me.

Pass me not, O gracious Father!
Lost and sinful though I be;
Thou might'st curse me, but the rather
Let Thy mercy light on me,
Even me.

Pass me not, O tender Saviour!
Let me love and cling to Thee:
Fain I'm longing for Thy favour;
When Thou callest, call for me,
Even me.

Pass me not, O mighty Spirit!
Thou canst make the blind to see;
Testify of Jesus' merit,
Speak the word of peace to me,
Even me.

Have I long in sin been sleeping,
Long been slighting, grieving Thee?
Has the world my heart been keeping?
Oh! forgive and rescue me,
Even me.

Love of God! so pure and changeless;
Love of Christ! so rich and free;
Grace of God! so strong and boundless,
Magnify it all in me,
Even me.

Pass me not, Almighty Spirit!
Draw this lifeless heart to Thee;
Impute to me the Saviour's merits;
Blessing others, oh! bless me,
Even me.

Then we must have faith in *a God of Purposeful Revival.* ". . . thou wilt revive me. . . . The Lord will perfect that which concerneth me: thy mercy, O Lord, endureth for ever: forsake not the works of thine own hands" (vss. 7a, 8). God's supreme purpose for your life and mine is perfection. That thought is taken up in the New Testament. Jesus said: "Be ye therefore *perfect,* even as your Father which is in heaven is perfect" (Matthew 5:48).

Paul declares that his object in preaching the gospel is that he might be able to present ". . . every man *perfect* in Christ Jesus" (Colossians 1:28). In another place he tells us that "All scripture is given by inspiration of God, and is profitable for doctrine, for reproof, for correction, for instruction in righteousness: That the man of God may be *perfect,* thoroughly furnished unto all good works" (II Timothy 3:16, 17). God's purpose in revival is that He might perfect us in His blessed Son, by the power of the Holy Spirit.

Faith in a God of personal revival, purposeful revival and *a God of Powerful Revival.* ". . . thou wilt *revive* me . . ." (vs. 7). The word "revive" means "to reanimate." In the great activities of God we read of His work in the realms of creation, re-creation and then of reanimation. When He created, He brought the first man into existence. When He re-creates, He brings the new man into being; but when there is backsliding, He sends revival to reanimate or revitalize. Have we the faith to believe God for this?

The text before us has yet one more lesson. It teaches that God revives men and women who are prepared to:

III EXPRESS BIBLICAL FORESIGHT IN THEIR LIVES

"Though I walk in the midst of trouble, thou wilt revive me: thou shalt stretch forth thine hand against the wrath of mine enemies, and thy right hand shall save me" (vs. 7). Anyone who knows his Bible recognizes that life for the Christian here upon earth is going to be confronted with tribulation and opposition. As we shall see in a moment, Jesus promised such times of testing and trial right through to the end of the journey. In the light of this, how important it is that the believer should face life in a state of spiritual revival.

Think for instance of *the Tribulation in the World.* Jesus said: "In the world ye shall have tribulation: but be of good cheer; I have overcome the world" (John 16:33). David is saying the same thing when he affirms, "Though I walk in the midst of trouble, thou wilt revive me . . ." (vs. 7). The child of God often can be revived *out* of trouble, more frequently revived *in* trouble, and repeatedly revived *through* trouble.

When the three youths, who knew the God of triumph, were in the fiery furnace, their persecutor, Nebuchadnezzar, had to say: "Lo, I see four men loose, walking in the midst of the fire, and they have no hurt; and the form of the fourth is like the Son of God" (Daniel 3:25). Conquest amidst the tribulations of life is the hallmark of genuine Christianity. The Christian is a man who acts victoriously and redemptively in every stress of life. O that the Lord would revive you and me until we triumph in the midst of trouble!

Then there is *the Opposition of the World.* In His Sermon on the Mount the Saviour taught: "Blessed are ye, when men shall revile you, and persecute you, and shall say all manner of evil against you falsely, for my sake. Rejoice, and be exceeding glad: for great is your reward in heaven: for so persecuted they the prophets which were before you" (Matthew 5:11, 12). And this is virtually what David is telling us in his psalm: ". . . thou shalt stretch forth thine hand against . . . mine enemies, and thy right hand shall save me" (vs. 7).

There was a day in the life of David when we read that he waxed faint and would have been slain by one of the sons of the giant, but Abishai came to his aid and smote the Philistine and saved David (II Samuel 21:15-17). Tell me, are you waxing faint in the battle against the Philistines? Is the opposition of the world too hot for you? Then ask the Lord to revive your experience of the heavenly Abishai that you might be able to conquer the enemies of your soul. The truly revived Christian can say and mean, "I am more than conqueror through Him that loved me" (Romans 8:37).

So we have seen the kind of people whom God is prepared to revive. They are the men and women who are ready to confess spiritual failure in their lives, whether it be prayerlessness, fearfulness or barrenness; people who are ready to profess practical faith in their lives in a God who revives personally, purposefully, and powerfully; people who are ready to express biblical foresight in their lives so as to be ready for tribulation or opposition when it comes. Will you pray, "Revive me," and then open your being to the Spirit of Revival, and do not rest until you have been restored to the fullness of the blessing that God is waiting to vouchsafe to you.

Lord, thou hast been favourable unto thy land: thou hast brought back the captivity of Jacob.
Thou hast forgiven the iniquity of thy people, thou hast covered all their sin. Selah.
Thou hast taken away all thy wrath: thou hast turned thyself from the fierceness of thine anger.
Turn us, O God of our salvation, and cause thine anger toward us to cease.
Wilt thou be angry with us for ever? wilt thou draw out thine anger to all generations?
Wilt thou not revive us again: that thy people may rejoice in thee?
Shew us thy mercy, O Lord, and grant us thy salvation.
I will hear what God the Lord will speak: for he will speak peace unto his people, and to his saints: but let them not turn again to folly.
Surely his salvation is nigh them that fear him; that glory may dwell in our land.
Mercy and truth are met together; righteousness and peace have kissed each other.
Truth shall spring out of the earth; and righteousness shall look down from heaven.
Yea, the Lord shall give that which is good; and our land shall yield her increase.
Righteousness shall go before him; and shall set us in the way of his steps.

PSALM 85

3

The "WHY" of Revival

"WILT THOU NOT REVIVE US AGAIN: THAT THY PEOPLE MAY rejoice in thee?" (Psalm 85:6). Here are words which help us to understand the nature of the purpose in revival, for, in answer to the "why," we have the psalmist's arresting reply: ". . . that thy people may rejoice in thee." Before we analyze verse 6, it is important that we give attention to the context.

In the first three verses the writer of this song is looking back to a previous revival. Notice his longing: "Lord, thou hast been favourable unto thy land: thou hast brought back the captivity of Jacob. Thou hast forgiven the iniquity of thy people, thou hast covered all their sin. Selah. Thou hast taken away all thy wrath: thou hast turned thyself from the fierceness of thine anger" (vss. 1-3). He is recalling the time when God delivered Israel from captivity, forgave the iniquity of the people and in sovereign grace restrained the fierceness of His anger.

In the verses that follow the psalmist forecasts the possibility of a great national revival to come. Implicit in his utterances, however, the inspired hymnist is laying down divine principles that determine a spiritual revival whenever God's people are ready in the day of His power.

The central message of this psalm is the answer to the question as to why God's people need a revival. There is a threefold answer to which we must give careful and prayerful attention. Revival is necessary in order to:

I RESTRAIN THE RIGHTEOUS ANGER OF GOD

"Turn us, O God of our salvation, and cause thine anger toward us to cease. Wilt thou be angry with us for ever? wilt thou draw out thine anger to all generations? Wilt thou not revive us again: that thy people may rejoice in thee?" (vss. 4-6). It is evident from these words that God reveals righteous anger against those of His people who live in *an Unrevived State.* "Wilt thou be angry with us for ever? wilt thou draw out thine anger to all generations? Wilt thou not revive us again: that thy people may rejoice in thee?" (vss. 5, 6). This unrevived state is vividly described to us in three words which significantly punctuate this psalm.

The first of these words is found in verse 2: "Thou hast forgiven the iniquity of thy people." *Iniquity* denotes wickedness, and the tragedy is that such wickedness can be found even in the heart of a redeemed man or woman. Every Christian is possessed of two natures—the old and the new. If he is living in the fullness of the Holy Spirit then the new nature is dominant and the old is dormant. On the other hand, if he is living in an unrevived state then this wickedness finds expression in subtle forms of iniquity. How true are the words of Jeremiah the prophet: "The heart is deceitful above all things, and desperately wicked: who can know it?" (17:9). Iniquity is that form of evil in our hearts which tries to explain away God's demands upon our lives in order that we may continue to sin.

In another place the psalmist says, "If I regard iniquity in my heart, the Lord will not hear me" (Psalm 66:18). Translated more literally this means that if I look with approval upon anything which is out of adjustment to the will of God the Lord will not hear me. Surely this explains why so often prayers are not heard, our service is not blessed, and our lives are so barren. We have explained away the divine commands and lowered the standards of God's expectation in our lives. This wickedness or iniquity in turn leads to what the psalmist plainly calls "sin"—". . . thou hast covered all their sin" (vs. 2).

The Apostle John tells us in his epistle that ". . . sin is the transgression of the law," or, as the Revised Standard Version puts it, ". . . sin is lawlessness" (I John 3:4). Wickedness always leads to lawlessness, or that arrogant violation of the will of God. Explain away the divine demands and it is an easy step to disobey them. How prevalent is this sin in the church of Jesus Christ today! Think of the sin of non-attendance at church gatherings (Hebrews 10:25); the sin of unreliability in Christian service (I Corinthians 4:2); the sin of unholiness in everyday life (I Thessalonians 4:7). On this latter point much could be said by way of illustration. Every thoughtful Christian must be aware of the fact that we are living in a day of so-called "double standards." A "philosophy of persuasion" is being used to interest thousands of our young people into ways of immorality, unchastity and then easy divorce. But the description does not end there. The psalmist goes on to say that wickedness produces lawlessness and this in turn leads to *carelessness*. This word is found in verse 8 where we read that God ". . . will speak peace unto his people, and to his saints: but let them not turn again to folly." How often we hear the expression, "I couldn't care less." Wickedness and lawlessness have produced an insensibility to evil and therefore a cold, calculated carelessness. And yet God has said, "The thought of foolishness is sin . . ." (Proverbs 24:9).

When I look into the faces of men and women who laugh and mock when God is speaking to them about iniquity and sin and folly, I can understand why God's righteous anger is revealed from heaven. God cannot condemn sin in the sinner and condone it in the saint. This is what Peter means when he says, "For the time is come that judgment must begin at the house of God . . ." (I Peter 4:17). We talk about the judgment of an evil world, but we forget that the risen Lord is Judge of His own church. As He walks amongst the candlesticks His eyes burn as flames of fire when He sees iniquity, sin and folly abounding (see Revelation 2).

God has a high standard for His church and His people, and we must not forget it. Consider for instance such utterances as these:

Thy testimonies are very sure: holiness becometh thine house, O Lord, for ever (*Psalm 93:5*).

Because it is written, Be ye holy; for I am holy (*I Peter 1:16*).

For God hath not called us unto uncleanness, but unto holiness (*I Thessalonians 4:7*).

God's anger is revealed not only against those who live in an unrevived state, but also against those who live in *an Unrepentant State*. "Turn us, O God of our salvation, and cause thine anger toward us to cease" (Psalm 85:4). It is one thing to be unrevived, but it is worse to be unrepentant. For too long now we have thought of the message of repentance only in terms of the unregenerate sinner, but we must remember that God calls His own people to repentance. If you have any doubt about this, get down on your knees and read solemnly chapters 2 and 3 of the Book of the Revelation. Speaking to the church, Jesus says:

. . . I will . . . remove thy candlestick out of his place, except thou repent (*Revelation 2:5*).

Repent; or else I will come unto thee quickly, and will fight. . . . with the sword of my mouth (*Revelation 2:16*).

Remember . . . how thou hast received and heard, and hold fast, and repent (*Revelation 3:3*).

. . . be zealous therefore, and repent (*Revelation 3:19*).

Yes, revival is needed in order to restrain the righteous anger of God. But in the second place revival is essential in order to:

II RESTORE THE CONSCIOUS AWARENESS OF GOD

"Wilt thou not revive us again: that thy people may rejoice in thee? Shew us thy mercy, O Lord, and grant us thy salvation. I will hear what God the Lord will speak: for he will speak peace unto his people, and to his saints: but let them not turn again to folly" (Psalm 85:6-8). Somebody has described revival as a person or a community saturated with the presence of God, and this is an accurate description; for when God breaks into a life or a community there is nothing else that matters save the person of Jesus, the glory of Jesus, the name of Jesus. Revival is not some emotion or worked-up excitement; it is rather an invasion from heaven which brings a conscious awareness of God. The psalmist describes it beautifully for us in this psalm.

To help you remember it let me put it in this form: the conscious awareness of God means *the smiling of His face.* "Wilt thou not revive us again . . . ?" (vs. 6). More literally this should read, "Wilt thou not *return* and revive us again?" It was an accepted fact amongst God's ancient people that when He was angry He turned His face away. On the other hand, when God came out to a repentant and restored people the picture in their minds was that of a smiling deity. This is the significance behind the threefold blessing pronounced by the priests upon the children of Israel in Numbers 6: "The Lord bless thee, and keep thee: The Lord make his face shine upon thee, and be gracious unto thee: The Lord lift up his countenance upon thee, and give thee peace" (vss. 24-26). The psalmist could also pray, "Make thy face to shine upon thy servant . . ." (Psalm 31:16). You remember that when Absalom was in disgrace he was told that he would not see the king's face for three years (II Samuel 13).

O that God would show us His face once again in the person of His beloved Son! Surely this is His purpose not only in the initial revelation of Himself to the human soul, but in the day-by-day communion which follows. Paul put it this way: "For God, who commanded the light to shine out of darkness, hath shined in our hearts, to give the light of the knowledge of the glory of God in the face of Jesus Christ" (II Corinthians 4:6).

Then there is also *the showing of His grace.* "Shew us thy mercy, O Lord, and grant us thy salvation" (vs. 7). The conscious awareness of God in the believer's life is a guarantee of the grace of victory. "For sin shall not have dominion over you: for ye are not under the law, but under grace" (Romans 6:14). Living in grace! That is the divine intention for each believing heart, but do we know this divine mercy and delivering grace day by day?

And if we have an awareness of God we will also know *the sounding of His voice.* "I will hear what God the Lord will speak: for he will speak peace unto his people, and to his saints: but let them not turn again to folly" (vs. 8). Every revival in history has been accompanied by a new recognition of the voice of God. The Bible lives and speaks again. Audiences are hushed under the sound of authoritative preaching.

I remember hearing the Reverend Duncan Campbell describe how preacher and listeners were hushed again and again in the presence of God during the Hebrides Revival. It was just as if God had broken into the situation with the words, "Be still, and know that I am God."

Revival, then, restores the conscious awareness of God amongst His people. But once more let us observe from the psalm that revival is essential in order to:

III REVEAL THE GRACIOUS ACTIVITIES OF GOD

"Surely his salvation is nigh them that fear him; that glory may dwell in our land. Mercy and truth are met together; righteousness and peace have kissed each other. Truth shall spring out of the earth; and righteousness shall look down from heaven. Yea, the Lord shall give that which is good; and our land shall yield her increase. Righteousness shall go before him; and shall set us in the way of his steps" (vss. 9-13).

Since the fall of man in the Garden of Eden there has never been a moment in time when God has not been active. Jesus put this plainly when He said, "My Father worketh hitherto, and I work" (John 5:17). He is active all over the world at this very hour.

The evidence that Christians by and large are not living in revival is that we do not see God at work. At a recent missionary conference I was impressed with the fact that although speaker after speaker reported enemy advance in practically every field of the world, there was notwithstanding a distinct note of victory concerning the triumphs of the gospel. When revival comes, it is as if a veil is lifted and we see God in action in the very areas where before we had seen nothing but darkness and defeat.

Arthur Wallis, in his book *In the Day of Thy Power,* illustrates this beautifully: "There was once an ancient reservoir in the hills that supplied a village community with water. It was fed by a mountain stream, and the overflow from the reservoir continued down the streambed to the valley below. There was nothing at all remarkable about this stream. It flowed on its quiet way without even disturbing the boulders that lay in its path or the foot-bridges that crossed it at various points. It seldom over-flowed its steep banks, or gave the villagers any trouble. One day, however, some large cracks appeared in one of the walls of the old reservoir, and soon afterwards the wall collapsed, and the waters burst forth down the hillside. They rooted up great trees; they carried along boulders like playthings; they destroyed houses and bridges and all that lay in their path. The streambed could not now contain the volume of water, which therefore flowed over the countryside, even inundating distant dwellings. What had before been ignored or taken for granted now became an object of awe and wonder and fear. From far and near people who in the usual way never went near the stream, hastened to see this great sight."

In picture language this is revival. At the present time God is at work, like that trickle of water, but when revival comes the trickle becomes a mighty deluge sweeping everything before it.

The activity of God in the world today is twofold. First there is *His saving activity.* "Surely his salvation is nigh them that fear him; that glory may dwell in our land" (vs. 9). God is saving men and women all over the world, but in proportion to the need it may seem like a little trickle. But if revival were to visit us the tens would become the hundreds, and the hundreds the thousands, and the thousands the millions. You only have to read the story of the great movements of the Spirit one hundred years ago in Great Britain and the United States to see what God did in a matter of months. O for another such visitation!

Next there is *His sanctifying activity.* This is evidenced in three ways. First, *in personal life.* "Mercy and truth are met together; righteousness and peace have kissed each other" (vs. 10). What a delightful description of a sanctified life! All those glorious qualities were gathered up in the nature and personality of our Lord Jesus. When He dwells in us in all revival fullness, all flesh can *see* the glory of God.

Oswald Chambers used to say, "Sanctification is allowing the perfections of the Lord Jesus to express themselves in human personality." God wants men and women in whom are married mercy, truth, righteousness and peace. "For the kingdom of God is not meat and drink; but righteousness, and peace, and joy in the Holy Ghost" (Romans 14:17).

In general life. "Truth shall spring out of the earth; and righteousness shall look down from heaven" (vs. 11). There is no great religious revival that has taken place which has not effected the most outstanding reforms. Indeed, someone has said that the secret connections between revival and the destiny of nations can be shown to be greater evolutions of history than the Gothic invasion.

Dr. F. B. Meyer once said that "there has never been a great religious revival without social and political reforms." In this regard we might point out that the abolition of slavery followed a revival. The end of child labor resulted from a revival. Indeed, before the Wesleys and Whitfield preached their flaming messages of revival and reform, people in England were working ninety hours a week. But as a direct consequence of this movement of the Spirit, sixty working hours became the standard, and the first trade unions, in all their purity, were organized. Also flowing like many streams from this spiritual revival were the well-known movements like the YMCA, the Salvation Army, missionary societies, and most of our charitable organizations and educational institutions. We could add to this slum clearance programs, Sunday school work, and a host of other honored and useful reforms in our religious, social and economic life. The historian Samuel Green says that "the whole temper of the English people was changed."

In material life. "Yea, the Lord shall give that which is good; and our land shall yield her increase" (vs. 12). The most prosperous and glorious periods in English and American history are associated directly with revival. Material advancement as well as the health of the people were fruits of those times of refreshing from the presence of the Lord. And so the psalmist concludes with the words: "Righteousness shall go before him; and shall set us in the way of his steps" (vs. 13). When the Lord our God moves through a land in revival blessing He lays out a pathway for His people to walk in and inevitably the nation follows, for "Righteousness exalteth a nation: but sin is a reproach to any people" (Proverbs 14:34). Conversely, where there is no vision the people throw off all moral restraint (Proverbs 29:18).

So we have sought to answer the question, "Why revival?" The answer is simple but, more than that, it is vital. Revival is absolutely essential to restrain the righteous anger of God, to restore the conscious awareness of God, and to reveal the gracious activity of God. In the light of these facts we are driven to pray again, "Wilt thou not revive us again: that thy people may rejoice in thee?"

In 1890 James Gilmour of Mongolia wrote to an old college friend: "You say you want reviving, go direct to Jesus and ask it straight-out, and you will get it straightaway. This revived state is not a thing you need to work yourself up into, or need others to help you rise into, or need to come to England to have operated upon you;—Jesus can effect it anywhere and does effect it everywhere whenever a man or woman, or men and women, ask it." ". . . ask, and ye shall receive . . ." (John 16:24).

Evan Roberts, who was so greatly used in the 1904 revival in Wales, bowed himself over a church pew and prayed, "O God, bend me, bend me, bend me," and God answered his longing heart and met him in such revival blessing as influenced the whole of the principality.

Are you prepared to ask for revival? Are you prepared to look for revival? Are you prepared to be broken in repentance and then bent to meet the divine conditions? If so, pray with the psalmist, "Wilt thou not revive us again . . . ?"

A prayer of Habakkuk the prophet upon Shigionoth.
O Lord, I have heard thy speech, and was afraid: O Lord, revive thy work in the midst of the years, in the midst of the years make known; in wrath remember mercy.
God came from Teman, and the Holy One from mount Paran. Selah. His glory covered the heavens, and the earth was full of his praise.
And his brightness was as the light; he had horns coming out of his hand: and there was the hiding of his power.
Before him went the pestilence, and burning coals went forth at his feet.
He stood, and measured the earth: he beheld, and drove asunder the nations; and the everlasting mountains were scattered, the perpetual hills did bow: his ways are everlasting.
I saw the tents of Cushan in affliction: and the curtains of the land of Midian did tremble.
Was the Lord displeased against the rivers? was thine anger against the rivers? was thy wrath against the sea, that thou didst ride upon thine horses and thy chariots of salvation?
Thy bow was made quite naked, according to the oaths of the tribes, even thy word. Selah. Thou didst cleave the earth with rivers.
The mountains saw thee, and they trembled: the overflowing of the water passed by: the deep uttered his voice, and lifted up his hands on high.
The sun and moon stood still in their habitation: at the light of thine arrows they went, and at the shining of thy glittering spear.
Thou didst march through the land in indignation, thou didst thresh the heathen in anger.
Thou wentest forth for the salvation of thy people, even for salvation with thine anointed; thou woundedst the head out

of the house of the wicked, by discovering the foundation unto the neck. Selah.

Thou didst strike through with his staves the head of his villages: they came out as a whirlwind to scatter me: their rejoicing was as to devour the poor secretly.

Thou didst walk through the sea with thine horses, through the heap of great waters.

When I heard, my belly trembled; my lips quivered at the voice: rottenness entered into my bones, and I trembled in myself, that I might rest in the day of trouble: when he cometh up unto the people, he will invade them with his troops.

Although the fig tree shall not blossom, neither shall fruit be in the vines; the labour of the olive shall fail, and the fields shall yield no meat; the flock shall be cut off from the fold, and there shall be no herd in the stalls:

Yet I will rejoice in the Lord, I will joy in the God of my salvation.

The Lord God is my strength, and he will make my feet like hinds' feet, and he will make me to walk upon high places. To the chief singer on my stringed instruments.

HABAKKUK 3

4

The "WHEN" of Revival

"O LORD, I HAVE HEARD THY SPEECH, AND WAS AFRAID: O Lord, revive thy work in the midst of the years, in the midst of the years make known; in wrath remember mercy" (Habakkuk 3:2). Habakkuk appears on the scene unannounced. Who he was, and of what family or tribe he was born we are not told. Neither do we know very much about the time of his ministry. But we gather from the character of his messages that he came later than Ezra and Nehemiah and the prophets Haggai and Zechariah. His name is obscure, though there are scholars who tell us that it denotes "ardent embracing" or "wrestling." There is no doubt that he was a man who wrestled with God. In place after place throughout his prophecy we find him interceding in prayer and stretching out in faith as he seeks to rend the heavens and bring down the revival that his people so desperately needed. In the text we have chosen for our starting point, Habakkuk answers the question concerning *the "when" of revival.* Implicit in what he says, he shows that the "when" of revival is associated with:

I GOD'S SOVEREIGNTY

"O Lord, revive thy work in the midst of the years . . ." (vs. 2). The sovereignty of God in a spiritual awakening is always demonstrated by *the manner of His working.* "O Lord, revive thy work . . ." (vs. 2). God is ever and always working. When here upon earth the Master could say, "My Father worketh hitherto, and I work" (John 5:17). It is in the very nature of God's activity to continue working until the task is completed. Only the sinfulness of man hinders the progress of the divine purpose. But notwithstanding all that man says or does, God will finish His work. The Apostle Paul expresses this beautifully in his word to the church at Philippi: "Being confident of this very thing, that he which hath begun a good work in you will perform it until the day of Jesus Christ" (Philippians 1:6).

In the passage which follows our text there is the most vivid description of the characteristics of God's activity in the ministry of revival. Consider them with me for a moment. When God works in reviving power He does so with *a suddenness.* "God came from Teman, and the Holy One from mount Paran. Selah. His glory covered the heavens, and the earth was full of his praise" (vs. 3). When the Holy Spirit came at Pentecost it was with "a suddenness," for we read: ". . . suddenly there came a sound from heaven as of a rushing mighty wind. . . . And they were all filled with the Holy Ghost, and began to speak with other tongues, as the Spirit gave them utterance" (Acts 2:2, 4). And how true it was that following this invasion from heaven the glory of God covered the heavens and the earth was full of His praise. For with the birth of the church and the spread of her witness, the sons of Zion passed from one city to another until the whole world was encompassed.

When God works in reviving power He also does so with *a searchingness.* "And his brightness was as the light; he had horns coming out of his hand: and there was the hiding of his power. Before him went the pestilence, and burning coals went forth at his feet" (vss. 4-5). It is significant that when the Holy Spirit came at Pentecost we read that He appeared as tongues of fire sitting upon each of the men and women gathered in the upper room (Acts 2:3). That fire symbolized not only the purity but the searchingness of God. It is little wonder that the preaching that followed Pentecost pricked men and women to the heart so that they cried out, "Men and brethren, what shall we do?" (Acts 2:37). Revival can never come without an exposure of and judgment on sin.

God also works in reviving power with *a solemness.* In verses 6 through 12 Habakkuk takes up instances from the lives of David, Deborah and Joshua to illustrate God's solemn dealings with His people in times past. He recalls how God marched through the land in indignation, and threshed the heathen in anger (vs. 12). Already Habakkuk has pointed out in his prophecy that God is ". . . of purer eyes than to behold evil . . ." (1:13). The prophet is only saying again that we cannot expect revival if we are not prepared to humble ourselves under the mighty hand of our God and accept His judgment upon every appearance of sin.

And finally, God works in reviving power with *a savingness.* "Thou wentest forth for the salvation of thy people, even for salvation with thine anointed; thou woundedst the head out of the house of the wicked, by discovering the foundation unto the neck" (3:13). In this picturesque and vivid language the prophet is describing the mighty saving activity which follows in the wake of revival. God's purpose is always redemptive in its outworking. So we have seen the manner of His sovereign working in revival.

But in our text we also have *the manner of His timing.* "O Lord, revive thy work in the midst of the years, in the midst of the years make known . . ." (vs. 2). Commentators have always found the phrase "in the midst of the years" difficult to interpret. But whatever connotation we may attach to these words, of one thing we can be clear: in the sovereign workings of God we can always be sure of *the divine revelation of the exact moment.* ". . . revive thy work in the midst of the years. . . ." When the Lord Jesus was about to leave for heaven His disciples requested that they might know when and where He would restore the kingdom to His ancient people. The Master replied, "It is not for you to know the times or the seasons, which the Father hath put in his own power" (Acts 1:7). Of one thing, however, they could be certain: that God always works on time. He did so when the heavens and the earth were created, for we read: "In the beginning God created the heaven and the earth" (Genesis 1:1). This was precision timing. At the coming of our Lord Jesus into the world God was again on time for it is recorded that ". . . when the fulness of the time was come, God sent forth his Son, made of a woman, made under the law" (Galatians 4:4). This was equally true on the occasion of the advent of the Holy Spirit, for Luke tells us: ". . . when the day of Pentecost was fully come . . . . suddenly there came a sound from heaven . . ." (Acts 2:1, 2). What a relief it is to know that God has planned the moment when to send revival. O that we might be ready in the day of His power!

In this matter of divine timing we can also be sure of *the divine revelation of the express message.* "O Lord, I have heard thy speech, and was afraid . . . in the midst of the years make known; in wrath remember mercy" (vs. 2). God not only times the moment for revival, but He invariably times the message for the spiritual awakening of the church. God has always said something definite and relevant to meet the contemporary need. We could illustrate this throughout the whole history of the Christian church, but let us start with the sixteenth century. This marked the Protestant revival or what is known as the Reformation. The message that rang out happens to be the very central word of Habakkuk: ". . . the just shall live by his faith" (2:4). Then came the seventeenth century with the revival of Puritanism. The messsage that time was the sovereignty of God and the responsibility of man. The eighteenth century saw the first evangelical awakening, with its restatement of the simple gospel of our Lord Jesus Christ. John Wesley and George Whitfield traveled north, south, east and west in the British Isles calling upon men and women to be born again and to be reconciled to God. The second evangelical awakening of the nineteenth century brought a slightly different emphasis. In a word it was to evangelize the world. There was a rediscovery of the meaning and mission of the Great Commission: to go ". . . into all the world, and preach the gospel to every creature" (Mark 16:15). Most of the well-established evangelical societies and foreign missions were born out of that revival. So we have seen something of the manner of God's sovereign working and timing in this strange activity of His, which we call revival.

But the "when" of revival has to do not only with God's sovereignty; it is also associated with:

II MAN'S EXTREMITY

"O Lord, revive thy work in the midst of the years, in the midst of the years make known; in wrath remember mercy" (vs. 2). Here is the longing of a man in dire straits. There is a burden upon his heart; there is a sob in his voice and there are tears in his eyes. He has reached an extremity.

As I have read and reread the stories of revivals, I have found that God always visits His people when they reach *the point of desperation.* Habakkuk opens his prophecy with the words, "The burden which Habakkuk the prophet did see" (1:1). Then follows a vision of the desperate condition of his people. He sees sin as high as the mountains, the law of God disregarded and the wicked compassing the righteous. In verses 5 to 11 of that first chapter God replies to the heart-cry of the prophet and discloses what He is about to do. So backslidden and wicked were the chosen people that God has to raise up a nation worse than themselves to whip them into submission and repentance. Listen to His language: "For, lo, I raise up the Chaldeans, that bitter and hasty nation, which shall march through the breadth of the land, to possess the dwellingplaces that are not theirs" (1:6). God has had to do this again and again throughout history. It makes me wonder if we are not reaching the point when it may well happen again. Communism, with all its strength and sinister and subtle strategy, is infiltrating one country after another. How soon will it be before the west is overrun and the church is driven underground and persecuted? With such a horrifying vision before him, Habakkuk cries out with words of utter desperation: "Art thou not from everlasting, O Lord my God, mine Holy One? we shall not die. O Lord, thou hast ordained them for judgment; and, O mighty God, thou hast established them for correction. Thou art of purer eyes than to behold evil, and canst not look on iniquity: wherefore lookest thou upon them that deal treacherously, and holdest thy tongue when the wicked devoureth the man that is more righteous than he?" (1:12, 13).

It is my conviction that we are never going to have revival until God has brought the church of Jesus Christ to a point of desperation. As long as Christian people can trust religious organization, material wealth, popular preaching, shallow evangelistic crusades and promotion drives, there will never be revival. But when confidence in the flesh is smashed, and the church comes to the realization of her desperate wretchedness, blindness and nakedness before God, then and only then will God break in. Yes, there must be the point of desperation, but there must also be *the point of intercession.* "I will stand upon my watch, and set me upon the tower, and will watch to see what he will say unto me, and what I shall answer when I am reproved" (2:1). Whether or not the "watch" was an actual structure with a prayer room, we do not know. In any case that is immaterial. What is important and plain is that Habakkuk had come to the point where he had to shut himself up with God. There was nothing else to do but to watch, pray and wait until God spoke a word from heaven. O that God would bring *us* to this place of intercession! We cannot think or talk, let alone taste of revival, without intercessory prayer. Indeed, the reason for an unrevived church in the last analysis is the sin of prayerlessness. Certainly there are individuals who are praying for revival, and God is graciously meeting them in blessing at the point of their need, but where are the prayer groups, where are the companies of intercessors, where are the churches that are united in an agonizing cry that God would rend the heavens and come down and cause the mountains of hindrance and sin and unbelief to flow before His presence? Yes, there is only one thing that will save us in this hour of desperation, and that is prayer.

When Habakkuk prayed in this fashion we read: "And the Lord answered me, and said, Write the vision, and make it plain upon tables, that he may run that readeth it" (2:2). And in the place of intercession God gave him a twofold vision. First, *the vision of the sinfulness of man.* From 2:3 through 2:19 God describes to His servant the utter sinfulness of man by pronouncing five terrifying woes. Such is the character of this unveiling of man's desperate need that Habakkuk is brought to the depths of despair. But this is always God's method: until we understand heaven's pronouncements upon human sinfulness, we shall never be serious in our praying for revival.

And secondly, *the vision of the holiness of God.* "But the Lord is in his holy temple: let all the earth keep silence before him" (2:20). Because man is what he is in his native defilement, he can only understand the sinfulness of man against the background of the holiness of God. We see this repeated again and again in holy Scripture. Think, for instance, of Isaiah where we find the prophet pronouncing woes upon all and sundry—but he is unaware of his own need until he catches a vision of the holiness of God in chapter 6. Then he bursts out, "Woe is me! for I am undone; because I am a man of unclean lips, and I dwell in the midst of a people of unclean lips: for mine eyes have seen the King, the Lord of hosts" (6:5). This then is where man's extremity brings him to a point of desperation and intercession because of human sinfulness and divine holiness. But in terms of revival, this in turn leads to what we shall call:

III FAITH'S OPPORTUNITY

"O Lord, revive thy work in the midst of the years . . ." (vs. 2). Until revival comes there is only one attitude for the man of God: a strong faith which *behaves righteously.* ". . . the just shall live by his faith" (2:4). Until God rains righteousness from heaven there is no other way to live. The Apostle Paul says the same thing in Romans 1, where he catches up the imperative of faith from the prophecy of Habakkuk. Listen again to his words: "For I am not ashamed of the gospel of Christ: for it is the power of God unto salvation to every one that believeth; to the Jew first, and also to the Greek. For therein is the righteousness of God revealed from faith to faith: as it is written, The just shall live by faith" (Romans 1:16, 17).

One of the determining factors in bringing about a church-wide revival is this righteous behavior—living with a determination to fulfill all of God's purposes in the power of a Spirit-filled life. This, of course, is not popular in our present age. Carnal Christians do not and will not understand this attitude to life. They look askance at you and say, "Why bother to live like that? Why be a martyr? Why be considered different or odd?" God have mercy on such thinking and questioning! The Word is clear: "The just shall live by faith." This constitutes not only the call to a faith which behaves righteously, but also to a faith which *believes rejoicingly*. How gloriously is the attitude to life described in Habakkuk 3:17 through 19. Read again this magnificent poetry: "Although the fig tree shall not blossom, neither shall fruit be in the vines; the labour of the olive shall fail, and the fields shall yield no meat; the flock shall be cut off from the fold, and there shall be no herd in the stalls: Yet I will rejoice in the Lord, I will joy in the God of my salvation. The Lord God is my strength, and he will make my feet like hinds' feet, and he will make me to walk upon high places." Dr. G. Campbell Morgan says that is the greatest and most priceless passage in the whole of prophetic poetry.

In verse 17 Habakkuk gives us a picture of a country laid waste. What a description of the present-day church! But faith, mighty faith, looks at a hopeless situation and laughs rejoicingly and victoriously. Yes, it does not matter how barren, how wasted, how fruitless may be the life of the church individually or corporately—God can save, restore and revive. Dr. Morgan points out that to translate this passage literally from the Hebrew would almost startle us. What Habakkuk is saying here is: "I will jump for joy in the Lord. I will spin round for joy in God." This is believing rejoicingly. This is faith looking beyond the desolation of sin to the consolation of the Spirit.

While the man of faith behaves righteously and believes rejoicingly, waiting for revival, his own life may be *energized.* "The Lord God is my strength . . ." (vs. 19). If we study the lives of men like Moses, Joshua, David, Isaiah and John, we shall see that despite the despairing human outlook God energized them to see the state and stand the strain until it was time for God to intervene. How wonderful to know that until God sends revival we can be individually energized.

His life may also be *stabilized.* ". . . he will make my feet like hinds' feet . . ." (vs. 19). The hind is one of the most sure-footed animals known to man. However dizzy the heights or precipitous the rocks, the hind is sure of its footing. When personal revival lifts us to those heights of revelation and experience, we need to be strengthened by God's Spirit in the inner man to stand the wonder and glory of the indwelling Son of God. How welcome it is to know that we can be ". . . stedfast, unmoveable, always abounding in the work of the Lord . . ." (I Corinthians 15:58). And further, a life may be *vitalized.* ". . . he will make me to walk upon high places" (vs. 19). It is one thing to stand; it is another to walk. By a glorious visitation from heaven a Christian can be placed on a pinnacle of fellowship with and fullness in Christ, but it is another thing to walk in that light and to continue to breathe that rarified atmosphere of heaven. But thank God, whether it is commencement or continuance in the Christian life, the secret is just the same. It is the faith of the just. The Apostle Paul puts it this way: "As ye have therefore received Christ Jesus the Lord, so walk ye in him" (Colossians 2:6).

We have seen that waiting for general revival is no excuse for not enjoying personal revival. Therefore, while we count upon the sovereignty of God, the extremity of man, and the opportunity of faith for a church-wide movement of the Spirit, we can in our individual lives behave righteously and believe rejoicingly through a faith that is energized, stabilized and vitalized by the Word of God and the Spirit of God. Only a Christian living on these terms has a right to pray, "O Lord, revive thy work in the midst of the years, in the midst of the years make known; in wrath remember mercy."

Now in the fifteenth year of the reign of Tiberius Caesar, Pontius Pilate being governor of Judaea, and Herod being tetrarch of Galilee, and his brother Philip tetrarch of Ituraea and of the region of Trachonitis, and Lysanias the tetrarch of Abilene,

Annas and Caiaphas being the high priests, the word of God came unto John the son of Zacharias in the wilderness.

And he came into all the country about Jordan, preaching the baptism of repentance for the remission of sins;

As it is written in the book of the words of Esaias the prophet, saying, The voice of one crying in the wilderness, Prepare ye the way of the Lord, make his paths straight.

Every valley shall be filled, and every mountain and hill shall be brought low; and the crooked shall be made straight, and the rough ways shall be made smooth;

And all flesh shall see the salvation of God.

LUKE 3:1-6

5

The "WAY" of Revival

"It was 1904. All Wales was aflame. The nation had drifted far from God. The spiritual conditions were low indeed. Church attendance was poor, and sin abounded on every side.

"Suddenly, like an unexpected tornado, the Spirit of God swept over the land. The churches were crowded, so that multitudes were unable to get in. Meetings lasted from ten in the morning until twelve at night. Three definite services were held each day. Evan Roberts was the human instrument, but there was very little preaching. Singing, testimony and prayer were the chief features. There were no hymnbooks, they had learned the hymns in childhood; no choir, for everybody sang; no collection, and no advertising.

"Nothing had ever come over Wales with such far-reaching results. Infidels were converted; drunkards, thieves and gamblers saved; and thousands reclaimed to respectability. Confessions of awful sins were heard on every side. Old debts were paid. The theater had to leave for want of patronage. Mules in coal mines refused to work, being unused to kindness! In five weeks, twenty thousand people joined the churches."

In this graphic manner, Dr. Oswald Smith tells us what happened when God swept through a country in revival blessing. Is it any wonder that we long to see another outpouring of God's Spirit? It is just here, however, that we must remind ourselves that such a longing must be tempered with the knowledge of the "way" of revival. Yes, there is a way of revival and it is a costly way—before we can see the salvation of God! That great reformer and revivalist, John the Baptist, put it this way: "Prepare ye the way of the Lord, make his paths straight. Every valley shall be filled, and every mountain and hill shall be brought low; and the crooked shall be made straight, and the rough ways shall be made smooth; And all flesh shall see the salvation of God" (Luke 3:4-6). With these words he summed up the conditions that are ever to determine the opportunity for God to work. If revival in terms of the full salvation of God is to be seen, then we must give attention to:

I WHAT IS ENJOINED

The challenge is: "Prepare ye the way of the Lord . . ." (vs. 4). In eastern lands, when an emperor or king was due to pass through the country, men were sent to prepare a highway for him. Isaiah and John borrow that figure to set forth what is enjoined in seeing revival. And so the word rings out: "Prepare ye the way of the Lord. . . ." Now if we are to catch the personal message in those words, we must first seek out the spiritual principles and then apply them to our personal lives.

When God says, "Prepare ye the way of the Lord," He is instructing us to be a means of access through which Christ can reveal Himself. So many of us are *obstructions* to Christ, and not *ways*. O that we might return to the simplicity and standard of the early Christians who were known as "the way"! Six times over in the Acts of the Apostles, Luke employed this term to identify the true followers of Christ. Even a poor demon-possessed girl had to exclaim, concerning Paul and Silas, "These men are the servants . . . which shew us . . . the way of salvation" (Acts 16:17). Can this be said of your life? In other words, "Is your life a way of *triumphant prayer*?" —or what the writer to the Hebrews calls ". . . the way into the holiest . . ." (Hebrews 9:8)? When people encounter you, are they ushered at once into the presence of God? Do other Christians find it easy to pray with you, or is your life a hindrance to prayer? Once again, is your life a way of *abundant life*—". . . a new and living way . . ." (Hebrews 10:20)? It is one thing to have life; it is quite another to enjoy abundant life. God's purpose for each believer is that he might ". . . reign in life by one, Jesus Christ" (Romans 5:17). Paul knew something of that experience when he wrote, "For to me to live is Christ . . ." (Philippians 1:21). And again, ". . . Christ . . . is our life . . ." (Colossians 3:4). May the Lord deliver us from merely existing and bring us into the joy of really living.

Then it might be asked, "Is your life a way of *consistent holiness?*"—". . . the way of righteousness . . ." (II Peter 2:21)? Holiness is not the privilege of the so-called aristocracy of heaven; rather it is the divine expectation and standard of everyone who names the name of Christ. The Word of God reminds us that ". . . this is the will of God, even your sanctification . . . ," and that we have not been ". . . called . . . unto uncleanness, but unto holiness" (I Thessalonians 4:3, 7). Peter puts it plainly when he says, ". . . as he which hath called you is holy, so be ye holy in all manner of conversation; Because it is written, Be ye holy; for I am holy" (I Peter 1:15-16). Was it not the saintly Robert Murray McCheyne who said the greatest ambition of his life was that he might be a holy man?

Perhaps the supreme question to ask is whether or not your life is a way of *transcendent love*—the ". . . more excellent way" (I Corinthians 12:31). We only have to study a passage like I Corinthians 13 to recognize that to have everything else but to be void of love is to be and to do nothing. It is said that Dr. Andrew Murray read this song of love every day on his knees before he attempted to preach or to serve his Lord in any way whatsoever. So the command is clear: "Prepare ye the way of the Lord . . ."—that is to say, become such a way of prayer, of life, of holiness and of love that all men shall see the salvation of God.

So we see what is enjoined in preparing the way, but now observe in the next place:

II WHAT IS ENTAILED

"Every valley shall be filled, and every mountain and hill shall be brought low; and the crooked shall be made straight, and the rough ways shall be made smooth" (Luke 3:5). John's mission was to prepare the way of the Lord by spiritually filling all the valleys, leveling the mountains, straightening the ways of crookedness and smoothing out the rough places. And in a similar manner, if we are to prepare the way of the Lord we shall have to face up to what is spiritually entailed. First, *the Valleys of Defeat must be filled.* "Every valley shall be filled. . . ." Valleys are depressions and divisions in the earth's surface, and as such symbolize aspects of defeat in the believer's life. There are the inward depressions. Their number is legion, but they can always be recognized by the fact that they keep the Christian in a state of depression. Some of the well-known ones are temper, jealousy, bitterness, resentment, moodiness, slavish fear and the inferiority complex. Then there are outward divisions. You know them so well: exclusivism, sectarianism and obscurantism. In a word, anything and everything that tends to break up the unity of the Spirit in the bond of peace. How tired we are of the exclusivism which neither welcomes nor extends fellowship to Christians outside its own circle; the sectarianism which claims to be the whole, while it is only a section of the church of Christ, and the obscurantism which refuses to see the other man's point of view, and pronounces judgment without justification. Are you defeated by these depressions and divisions in your life? Remember they are the valleys which must be filled up if the way is to be prepared for revival and salvation.

You may well ask, "How can the valleys in my life be filled?" The answer is, "By the Holy Spirit." The Word of God exhorts, ". . . be filled with the Spirit" (Ephesians 5:18). It is only when the Holy Ghost fills the life of a believer that the depressions are mastered and the divisions are mended.

Preparing the way of the Lord certainly entails the filling up of the valleys, but further, *the Mountains of Disbelief must be leveled.* ". . . every mountain and hill shall be brought low. . . ." Clearly the mountains in this connection speak of disbelief. It was to illustrate the presence of such disbelief in the hearts of His disciples that Jesus used the Jewish figure of speech, "removing mountains by faith." The mountains were not the objective, material ones, but the subjective and moral ones (Matthew 17:20)—the mountains in your life and mine that are holding back the blessing. Jesus said that there was only one measure to level such mountains of disbelief and that was and is ". . . faith as a grain of mustard seed. . . ." To exercise such faith as a grain of mustard seed is to acknowledge deliberately and honestly our utter smallness, weakness and uselessness apart from God.

Unbelief springs from pride, and until we are humbled God can never exalt us in blessing. So Peter tells us, ". . . God resisteth the proud, and giveth grace to the humble. Humble yourselves therefore under the mighty hand of God, that he may exalt you in due time" (I Peter 5:5-6). If we are not prepared to humble ourselves, God has to do it, and it is a fearful thing to have to fall into the hands of the living God. One of the most sobering chapters to read is Daniel 4. It is the story of a man called Nebuchadnezzar who lifted up himself in pride before God, claiming that he had brought about his own greatness and fame. Listen to his language: "Is not this great Babylon, that I have built for the house of the kingdom by the might of my power, and for the honour of my majesty?" (vs. 30). And the record goes on to say, "While the word was in the king's mouth, there fell a voice from heaven, saying, O king Nebuchadnezzar, to thee it is spoken; The kingdom is departed from thee. And they shall drive thee from men, and thy dwelling shall be with the beasts of the field: they shall make thee to eat grass as oxen, and seven times shall pass over thee, until thou know that the most High ruleth in the kingdom of men, and giveth it to whomsoever he will. The same hour was the thing fulfilled upon Nebuchadnezzar: and he was driven from men, and did eat grass as oxen, and his body was wet with the dew of heaven, till his hairs were grown like eagles' feathers, and his nails like birds' claws" (vss. 31-33).

After seven years, having learned his lesson and being restored to sanity and dignity, Nebuchadnezzar was able to say, "Now I . . . praise and extol and honour the King of heaven, all whose works are truth, and his ways judgment: and *those that walk in pride he is able to abase*" (vs. 37).

Yes, the mountains of disbelief and pride must be leveled. But that is not all. *The Crooked Ways of Dishonesty must be straightened.* "The crooked shall be made straight." The dishonesties of life must be faced. Think, for a moment, of the dishonesty of lying; that is, any species of designed deception. How many times a day do you lie in thought, word or deed? Then there is the dishonesty of hypocrisy—pretending to be what you are not in your prayers, confessions, testimony and life. Another serious dishonesty is that of thieving, or robbing God of energy, misspent money and squandered hours. These crooked ways of dishonesty must be straightened, and the time to do it is now. The Bible says, "If we confess our sins, he is faithful and just to forgive us our sins, and to cleanse us from all unrighteousness" (I John 1:9). Will you confess and forsake lying, hypocrisy, and thieving in your life? This is the way of revival.

Then God says to us: *the Rough Places of Dislocation must be made smooth.* "The rough ways shall be made smooth." The word "dislocation" means "to make the strata discontinuous," or "to be out of place," and this is most suggestive, for among other things it carries a challenge: "Are you out of place or out of adjustment to the will of God in relation to your personal life?" Nobody else knows about this but God and yourself. It is the kind of life you live behind closed doors when you are away from the crowd or your own people. Are you out of adjustment to the will of God in relation to your family life? What about the husband-wife relationship? Husband, are you lovingly considerate of your wife? Wife, are you lovingly submissive to your husband? What about the parent-children relationship? Parents, are you bringing up your children in the nurture and admonition of the Lord, not provoking them to anger or losing respect through lack of anointed authority, example and precept? Children, are you obeying your parents in the Lord by honoring your father and mother?

Then I am bound to ask, are you out of adjustment to the will of God in relation to your church life? Do you pray for your minister? Are you in harmony with fellow elders, deacons and members within the fellowship of your local church? Are you fulfilling your obligations in terms of attendance, service, giving and witness?

Then there is the social life. Are you out of adjustment to the will of God in this regard? Who are your friends?—schismatic Christians, or those who are walking in a disorderly fashion, or maybe unconverted people who have no love or time for the things of God? Have you never read the Word which says, ". . . if any man obey not our word . . . note that man, and have no company with him, that he may be ashamed" (II Thessalonians 3:14)?

And then concerning the world, James warns us, ". . . whosoever therefore will be a friend of the world is the enemy of God" (James 4:4). And again, "Be ye not unequally yoked together with unbelievers: for what fellowship hath righteousness with unrighteousness? and what communion hath light with darkness? And what concord hath Christ with Belial? or what part hath he that believeth with an infidel? . . . Wherefore come out from among them, and be ye separate, saith the Lord, and touch not the unclean thing: and I will receive you" (II Corinthians 6:14, 15, 17).

These principles apply also to your business life. God alone knows what would happen in the professional, commercial and industrial areas of our national life if He truly visited us with revival. What adjustments would be made!

Some while ago there was a spiritual awakening in South Africa, and we are told that the police authorities were astounded at the genuine repentance and restitutions that were made not only by converts, but by backsliders who were now restored to the Lord. The *Daily Dispatch* of East London, South Africa, listed the following articles returned by repentant believers: "80 sheets, 25 blankets, 24 jackets, 34 trousers, 11 overcoats, 6 women's coats, 25 dresses, 27 skirts, 50 shirts, 22 bedspreads, 64 hats, 23 towels, 1 table, 4 chairs, 50 pillow slips, 15 scissors, 5 hairclippers, 9 wallets, 4 cameras, 4 wrist watches, 3 revolvers and ammunition, 30 tumblers and an assortment of jewelry, tools, cigarette lighters, crockery, cutlery, boots and shoes, pressure stoves, frying pans, lanterns, and safety razors."

We are told that during a religious awakening in the city of Belfast, under the ministry of the Reverend W. P. Nicholson, there was such a spirit of repentance and restitution abroad that workers at a well-known shipyard returned sufficient material to the authorities to build and equip a sizable machine shed.

So we are bound to ask in these days of unprincipled business methods and neglected ethics, "Are you out of adjustment in relation to your business life?" Until you get right with God, He will not hear you or bless you. In whatever area of maladjustment, we must remember the solemn words of David: "If I regard iniquity in my heart, the Lord will not hear me" (Psalm 66:18).

There is only one way back into adjustment to the will of God. It is summed up for us in the words of our risen Lord in His address to the church at Ephesus: "Remember . . . from whence thou art fallen, and *repent*, and do the first works . . ." (Revelation 2:5).

These are certainly four heavy demands, but they constitute what is entailed in preparing the way of the Lord. This is the way of revival. Nothing else will do. On the other hand, if we are prepared to fill what is entailed, then we can proceed to:

III WHAT IS EXPECTED

". . . all flesh shall see the salvation of God" (vs. 6). If you look at Luke 2:30, you will notice that the salvation of God is embodied in a Person, even the Lord Jesus Christ Himself. When the godly Simeon lifted the infant Christ into his arms, he declared, "Lord, now lettest thou thy servant depart in peace, according to thy word: For mine eyes have seen thy salvation" (Luke 2:29-30). Revival is not an idea; still less is it mere emotion or excitement. Revival is ultimately Christ Himself, seen, felt and heard in and through His body on earth. He can only be seen by all flesh when the conditions are fulfilled. The way must be prepared and all flesh shall see the salvation of God. Notice what this means.

First, *unlimited blessing,* ". . . all flesh . . ." (vs. 6). In these two words God catches us up into His world-wide vision. He delivers us from a narrow, parochial, and "four-walled" outlook. Instead of being restricted to "our little flock," our interests and blessing reach out to all flesh.

Secondly, *unmistakable blessing,* ". . . all flesh *shall see* . . ." (vs. 6). There are always "signs following" when the risen Saviour has the right of way through individuals and churches. There is no mistaking it when God starts to work, for men and women are either antagonized by, or attracted to, but never neutralized by Christ. And when this happens there is no need to be always hiding behind the well-known formula: "Eternity alone will reveal the results."

Thirdly, there is *unspeakable blessing,* ". . . all flesh shall see *the salvation of God*" (vs. 6). This, as we have already observed, is the Lord Jesus Christ Himself, God's "Unspeakable Gift"—glorified and magnified amongst men. So the challenge rings out: "Prepare ye the way of the Lord. . . . And all flesh shall see the salvation of God." Accept what is enjoined, fulfill what is entailed, and you will have what is expected. *Prepare* . . . and you will see!

Have you read *By My Spirit,* by Jonathan Goforth? If not, do so. It is the story of a great revival which swept Korea and China in 1906-7. The blessing began when a man was ready to prepare the way of the Lord, at all costs. The man's name was Goforth. The great moment in his life was when he came across a statement by Charles Finney, which said that it was useless for Christians to expect revival by simply asking for it, without bothering to fulfill the laws which govern spiritual blessing. As soon as Goforth read these words, he said, "If Finney's right, then I am going to find out what these laws are and obey them, no matter what it costs." What do you think was the first law he discovered?—the very one he was not prepared to obey, namely being reconciled to a fellow-missionary! But God bound him to that law until he was prepared to obey. When he did, the clouds burst and revival flooded his life and everyone he touched.

The vital question which arises out of this story is: What law of spiritual revival are you disobeying? Can you say and mean:

Saviour I yield, long to be healed
  Praying Thee now to receive me:
Searching my heart, bid to depart
  Everything there that would grieve Thee.

R. HUDSON POPE

And when they were come in, they went up into an upper room, where abode both Peter, and James, and John, and Andrew, Philip, and Thomas, Bartholomew, and Matthew, James the son of Alphaeus, and Simon Zelotes, and Judas the brother of James.

These all continued with one accord in prayer and supplication, with the women, and Mary the mother of Jesus, and with his brethren.

And when the day of Pentecost was fully come, they were all with one accord in one place.

And suddenly there came a sound from heaven as of a rushing mighty wind, and it filled all the house where they were sitting.

And there appeared unto them cloven tongues like as of fire, and it sat upon each of them.

And they were all filled with the Holy Ghost, and began to speak with other tongues, as the Spirit gave them utterance.

Now when they heard this, they were pricked in their heart, and said unto Peter and to the rest of the apostles, Men and brethren, what shall we do?

Then Peter said unto them, Repent, and be baptized every one of you in the name of Jesus Christ for the remission of sins, and ye shall receive the gift of the Holy Ghost.

Then they that gladly received his word were baptized: and the same day there were added unto them about three thousand souls.

ACTS 1:13-14; 2:1-4, 37, 38, 41

6

The "WIND" of Revival

PENTECOST WILL EVER BE ASSOCIATED, IN TIME AND ETERNITY, with the wind of God. Peter dramatically described the moment and movement of that wind in the familiar words of Acts 2: "And when the day of Pentecost was fully come, they were all with one accord in one place. And suddenly there came a sound from heaven as of a rushing mighty wind, and it filled all the house where they were sitting" (vss. 1-2).

Again and again throughout Scripture the sovereign operation of the Holy Spirit is likened to the wind. Think, for instance, of the words of God to the prophet Ezekiel when He bade him: "Prophesy unto the wind, prophesy, son of man, and say to the wind, Thus saith the Lord God; Come from the four winds, O breath, and breathe upon these slain, that they may live" (Ezekiel 37:9).

Then we love to recall that evening scene when Jesus talked with the puzzled theologian, Nicodemus. To illustrate the point the Master was making with regard to the work of the Holy Spirit within the human personality, Jesus used a phenomenon ready at hand. Doubtless at the moment that He was speaking the light evening breezes were playing on their faces or sighing in the trees, and the Lord said, "The wind bloweth where it listeth, and thou hearest the sound thereof, but canst not tell whence it cometh, and whither it goeth: so is every one that is born of the Spirit" (John 3:8).

There is a suddenness, searchingness and sovereignty about the wind of God's Spirit, and that is why we can speak of "the wind of revival." I once heard that prince of expositors, Dr. G. Campbell Morgan, make this remark: "We cannot organize revival, but we can set our sails to catch the wind from heaven when God chooses to blow upon His people once again." The question arises as to what we mean by "setting our sails." I want to suggest, from the verses before us, that setting our sails for the wind of revival involves Preparation, Supplication and Expectation.

I PREPARATION

"And when the day of Pentecost was fully come, they were all with one accord in one place" (2:1). The Lord Jesus, before He went to the cross, told His disciples to go to Jerusalem and tarry there until they were endued with power from on high. His actual words were: ". . . behold, I send the promise of my Father upon you: but tarry ye in the city of Jerusalem, until ye be endued with power from on high" (Luke 24:49).

And in obedience to that command they went into the city, to an upper room, to wait upon God. In every sense of the word this was a period of preparation. It involved *a oneness of mind*. ". . . they were all with one accord in one place" (2:1). Eleven times in the New Testament and on ten occasions in the Book of the Acts we read that they "were of one accord." This unity of mind seems to be an essential factor in the process of preparation for the wind of revival.

Some time ago I read through Dr. Edwin Orr's *Second Evangelical Awakening in Britain.* It is a magnificent work which covers the revivals that swept the British Isles some one hundred years ago. Analyzing the substance of his entire treatment, I came to the conclusion that the two outstanding conditions for revival are unity and prayer. In the beautiful Psalm 133 we read: "Behold, how good and how pleasant it is for brethren to dwell together in unity!" (vs. 1). And having stated that fact, the psalmist goes on to say, "It is like the precious ointment upon the head, that ran down upon the beard, even Aaron's beard: that went down to the skirts of his garments" (vs. 2). Then, changing the analogy, the hymnist continues, "As the dew of Hermon, and as the dew that descended upon the mountains of Zion: for there the Lord commanded the blessing, even life for evermore" (vs. 3).

What is the Holy Spirit saying to us in this psalm? Is it not that if we want the fragrance, freshness and fullness of spiritual revival, then it will only be as we dwell together in unity? Remember that high priestly prayer of our Lord's when He looked into His Father's face and said, "pray I. . . . That they all may be one; as thou, Father, art in me, and I in thee, that they also may be one in us . . ." (John 17:20, 21). Yes, it is only when God's people come together in oneness of mind that heaven opens and the wind of revival begins to blow upon the church on earth.

In this work of preparation there was also *an openness of heart*. A self-examination was carried out in that upper room. They rehearsed from the Scriptures and experience the sad and tragic story of Judas, the traitor in the camp, the man who ministered with them, who walked with the Saviour, who held the treasury, and yet whose heart was not perfect before God. In their attempt to find a successor to him, they prayed, "Thou, Lord, which knowest the hearts of all men, shew whether of these two thou hast chosen, That he may take part of this ministry and apostleship, from which Judas by transgression fell, that he might go to his own place" (Acts 1:24, 25). It was a prayer for searching, for examination, for judgment. There was an openness of heart, and God will never send revival blessing while there is sin unconfessed, while hearts are closed to the blaze of His glory and to the light that reveals evil. Before the Lord Jesus could minister the living waters to the woman of Samaria (John 4) He had to probe deep into her heart and expose sin. Until she was cleansed she could not receive the water of the Spirit.

Leafing over the first four chapters of the Acts of the Apostles you will find that in chapter 2 the disciples were filled with the Holy Ghost; but by the time we reach chapter 4 it is evident that something had happened. The fearlessness and faithfulness that characterized the early preaching have almost disappeared. Indeed, there is every evidence that the disciples were trembling and cringing before the magistrates and those who had become hostile to them. The explanation, of course, is that they had lost the fullness of the Spirit, and consequently their boldness and power. But those wise men quickly confessed their failure, and we read that once again the place was shaken and the Holy Spirit filled the building and those who were kneeling in prayer so that they could rise to go forth and speak the Word of God with boldness.

In chapter 5 sin enters the camp yet again through the presence of Ananias and Sapphira. Those people had tried to emulate Barnabas, the Spirit-filled man, who gave his all to the Lord; but there was duplicity in their hearts and defilement upon their hands. Peter, however, detected their deceit and judged it in the fear of God and in the presence of the church. It is recorded that great fear, great grace and great power came down upon the Christian assembly, and signs and wonders were done by the apostles and many believed on the name of Jesus, and the wind of revival was felt once again.

One of the functions of a strong wind is to cleanse and purify. It blows away pestilence and disease. Many times we have witnessed clouds, rain and even fog blown away by the strong wind from heaven. How important it is to be in the current of God's wind.

So we see that preparation involves a oneness of mind, an openness of heart, but it also calls for *an obedience of will.* Those 120 disciples gathered in the upper room were fulfilling the command of the Master, who said, ". . . tarry ye in the city of Jerusalem, until ye be endued with power from on high" (Luke 24:49).

Obedience is always a prerequisite to the filling and flooding of the Holy Spirit. The Word tells us that the Holy Ghost is given to those who obey Him (Acts 5:32). Charles Finney says that "a revival is nothing else than a new beginning of obedience to God. Just as in the case of a converted sinner, the first step is a deep repentance, a breaking down of heart, a getting down to the dust before God with deep humility and a forsaking of sin."

Are you longing for revival? Are you praying for the wind of God to blow upon the church of Jesus Christ? Then what about setting your sails by way of preparation to catch that heavenly breeze? Remember that it will involve a oneness of mind, an openness of heart and an obedience of will.

The second word which sums up the adjustment of our souls to the wind of God is:

II SUPPLICATION

"These all continued with one accord in prayer and supplication . . ." (1:14). There was nothing spasmodic or intermittent about their praying. On the contrary, there was *a constancy in prayer*. "These all continued . . . in prayer and supplication . . ." (1:14). Prayer is rarely mentioned in the Word of God without an emphasis on continuance. Jesus said, ". . . men ought always to pray, and not to faint" (Luke 18:1). The Apostle Paul exhorts us to "Pray without ceasing" (I Thessalonians 5:17).

Prayer is not only an activity, but an attitude of life. If we would pray always and without ceasing, then our whole life should be one continuous prayer ever open to heaven for whatever God would say or send. So many people imagine that prayer is the overcoming of the reluctance of God to give; whereas, in point of fact, prayer is the adjustment of our lives to God's will in order that He might be able to send the blessing He is waiting and longing to vouchsafe to His people. Bishop Lightfoot says, "It is not the moving of the lips, but in the elevation of the heart to God that the essence of prayer consists"—and it is surely in this sense that we are to put into practice the injunction to "Pray without ceasing."

Dr. Leon Morris remarks, "It is not possible for us to spend all our time with the words of prayer on our lips, but it is possible for us to be all our days in the spirit of prayer, realizing our dependence upon God for all that we have and are, realizing something of His presence with us wherever we may be, and yielding ourselves continually to Him for the doing of His will. Where there is such an inward state, it will find outward expression in verbal prayer, and in this connection we should notice the frequent ejaculatory prayers throughout Paul's letters. Prayer was so natural and so continual with the great Apostle that it found its way inevitably into his correspondence."

A unity in prayer. "These all continued with one accord in prayer . . ." (Acts 1:14). We have already spoken of the importance of unity in mind and in heart, but this must be carried into our prayer life as well. Jesus said, ". . . if two of you shall agree on earth as touching any thing that they shall ask, it shall be done for them of my Father which is in heaven" (Matthew 18:19). Have you ever put that to the test?

Dr. James Little tells the story of the 1857 revival in New York City and area. There was a man whose innermost soul was moved with a deep longing for an outpouring of the Spirit in that great city. The spiritual land around him was arid and parched, and his cry was, "Turn again our captivity, O Lord, as the streams in the south" (Psalm 126:4). Desiring that others should join him in concerted prayer, he displayed a little card in the window of a room on Fulton Street which read: "If anyone is interested to pray for revival, come in and join me." The first day he prayed alone. Then others began to join him, until the room became too small. The burden for revival had begun to spread—until hundreds had caught the spirit of intercession and supplication. Dr. Little relates that, very soon after, the winds of God began to blow and 250,000 souls were swept into the Kingdom in a few weeks.

Four young men in County Antrim, Northern Ireland, knelt likewise in united prayer in a schoolroom. They longed for revival and prayed for revival, and God met them in such a way that the whole of Ireland was affected. Indeed, that was the beginning of the 1859 revival that has influenced the country ever since.

Other instances could be cited to prove the point, if proof were needed, that God honors unity in prayer. But in addition to this, there must be *a fervency in prayer*. "These all continued with one accord in prayer and supplication . . ." (1:14). Prayer is a general connotation for waiting upon God, whereas the word "supplication" suggests the beseeching and petitioning aspect of intercession. It is the laying hold of the Lord which will not let go or let up until something happens. This is the way Elijah prayed, and James in citing this man of prayer writes: "The effectual fervent prayer of a righteous man availeth much" (James 5:16).

This kind of praying costs for it involves fasting, discipline and persistency. Luke recorded a prayer meeting of this kind in the twelfth chapter of the Book of the Acts. We read that ". . . prayer was made without ceasing of the church unto God . . ." for the imprisoned Peter. Such was the fervency and faithfulness of the praying that before the night was out Peter was delivered from his prison cell and released to preach the gospel of Christ. Are we prepared to set our sails by this ministry of supplication with constancy, unity and fervency? Only then can we expect to hear the mighty rushing wind from heaven.

One other thought in this story of Pentecost is gathered up for us in the word:

III EXPECTATION

"And when the day of Pentecost was fully come, they were all with one accord in one place. And suddenly there came a sound from heaven as of a rushing mighty wind, and it filled all the house where they were sitting. And there appeared unto them cloven tongues like as of fire, and it sat upon each of them. And they were all filled with the Holy Ghost, and began to speak with other tongues, as the Spirit gave them utterance" (Acts 2:1-4).

We can pray all night and all day throughout the coming weeks, and appear outwardly keen, but if there is no expectancy in our hearts there will be no blessing. A man said to me some time ago that he believed that God could stem the tide of evil, but he didn't have the faith to expect it. It never occurred to him that this was a contradiction of terms.

The characteristics of true expectation are threefold: first, *a faith that believes.* Jesus had said to His disciples, ". . . I send the promise of my Father upon you . . ." (Luke 24:49). They believed the promise. Indeed, one can sense the spirit of expectancy which characterized them as they knelt in prayer in that upper room. We also must exercise the faith which believes. Jesus said, ". . . all things, whatsoever ye shall ask in prayer, believing, ye shall receive" (Matthew 21:22). James reminds us that we are to ". . . ask in faith, nothing wavering: for he that wavereth is like a wave of the sea driven with the wind and tossed. For let not that man think that he shall receive any thing of the Lord" (James 1:6-7). ". . . faith cometh by hearing, and hearing by the word of God," declares the Apostle Paul (Romans 10:17).

There are a multitude of promises in the Old and New Testaments that give us the confidence to believe that God is waiting to send revival. One example will suffice. "Be patient . . . ," says the Apostle James, "unto the coming of the Lord. Behold, the husbandman waiteth for the precious fruit of the earth, and hath long patience for it, until he receive the early and latter rain" (James 5:7). Do we believe that the latter rain of revival is to fall before Jesus comes back again? The promise is clear enough, but is our faith strong enough? Is it a faith which believes?

Expectancy also calls for *a faith which receives.* ". . . they were all filled with the Holy Ghost . . ." (Acts 2:4). God fills only the hearts and lives of those who have a receiving faith. Have you received this fullness? God's purpose for our lives is continuous revival, and continuous revival is equated with the continuous fullness of the Holy Spirit. When we are first converted the word to us is: "Repent, and be baptized every one of you in the name of Jesus Christ for the remission of sins, and ye shall *receive the gift of the Holy Ghost*" (Acts 2:38). From that point onward the relevant exhortation is Ephesians 5:18: ". . . but be filled with the Spirit." Have we the faith to receive the fullness which God is waiting to pour out?

Expectation calls for yet another expression of faith—*a faith that achieves*. We read: ". . . they were all filled with the Holy Ghost, and began to speak . . . as the Spirit gave them utterance. . . . the same day there were added unto them about three thousand souls" (vss. 4, 41). Filled with the Holy Ghost, speaking with fearlessness, they stepped out to achieve results for God. And their expectation was not unrewarded. A large city was shaken, a great crowd was challenged and three thousand souls were converted in one day. Their whole ministry carried a relevance, an authority and a conviction such as men and women had never before heard. What happened on the day of Pentecost continued to happen throughout succeeding days and weeks, for we read that ". . . the Lord added to the church daily such as should be saved" (2:47). That is to say, men and women got right with God; not only on Sundays or on special preaching occasions, but every day, in homes, in the synagogue, in the market place and wherever unconverted men and women came into contact with those Spirit-filled, revived men and women.

So we have seen that our part in revival is to adjust the sails of our spiritual life to catch the first breeze that comes from heaven. Such adjustment involves preparation, supplication and expectation; or to put it in the words of Bessie P. Head, we ought thoughtfully and longingly to sing:

O Breath of Life, come sweeping through us,
Revive Thy Church with life and pow'r;
O Breath of Life, come, cleanse, renew us,
And fit Thy Church to meet this hour.

O Wind of God, come bend us, break us,
Till humbly we confess our need;
Then in Thy tenderness remake us,
Revive, restore, for this we plead.

O Breath of Love, come breathe within us,
Renewing thought and will and heart;
Come, Love of Christ, afresh to win us,
Revive Thy Church in every part.

And as they spake unto the people, the priests, and the captain of the temple, and the Sadducees, came upon them,

Being grieved that they taught the people, and preached through Jesus the resurrection from the dead.

And they laid hands on them, and put them in hold unto the next day: for it was now eventide.

Howbeit many of them which heard the word believed; and the number of the men was about five thousand.

Now when they saw the boldness of Peter and John, and perceived that they were unlearned and ignorant men, they marvelled; and they took knowledge of them, that they had been with Jesus.

And beholding the man which was healed standing with them, they could say nothing against it.

But when they had commanded them to go aside out of the council, they conferred among themselves,

Saying, What shall we do to these men? for that indeed a notable miracle hath been done by them is manifest to all them that dwell in Jerusalem; and we cannot deny it.

But that it spread no further among the people, let us straitly threaten them, that they speak henceforth to no man in this name.

And they called them, and commanded them not to speak at all nor teach in the name of Jesus.

But Peter and John answered and said unto them, Whether it be right in the sight of God to hearken unto you more than unto God, judge ye.

For we cannot but speak the things which we have seen and heard.

So when they had further threatened them, they let them go, finding nothing how they might punish them, because of the people: for all men glorified God for that which was done.

ACTS 4:1-4, 13-21

7

The "WAKE" of Revival

SOMETHING OF SUCH FAR-REACHING CONSEQUENCE HAD TAKEN place in Jerusalem that everyone in the city was aware of it. The Spirit of God had been poured out upon a handful of men and women, and, as a result, the very foundations of hell had been shaken. Never had such miraculous happenings been witnessed. On the day of Pentecost some three thousand souls had been added to the infant church. A few days later five thousand more were converted, and then still another five thousand until Luke, in his record, had to give up counting and by way of report used the term "myriads" to represent the multitudes who were turning to the Lord. Nothing quite like it has ever been achieved since. The enemies of the cross had to stand back and say, "What shall we do to these men? . . . that it spread no further among the people, let us straitly threaten them, that they speak henceforth to no man in this name. And they called them, and commanded them not to speak at all nor teach in the name of Jesus. But Peter and John answered and said unto them, Whether it be right in the sight of God to hearken unto you more than unto God, judge ye. For we cannot but speak the things which we have seen and heard" (Acts 4:16-20). The antagonists of the gospel had to acknowledge that "something was spreading—and spreading fast." Little did they know that it was the "wake" of revival.

This is our supreme need today, and we must not be satisfied with anything less. Our study of God's Word, our ministry in prayer, our holiness of living and our devotion in service must all be directed to this end, until our enemies have to say, ". . . that it spread no further among the people, let us straitly threaten them, that they speak henceforth to no man in this name" (vs. 17).

What we must discover at once is:

I WHAT ARE THE SECRETS OF SPREADING REVIVAL?

I believe all the secrets are summed up in that most significant little statement tucked away in verse 13: ". . . they had been with Jesus." Revival in the last analysis—whether praying, praising or preaching—is Jesus. It is the manifestation of the glory, power and blessing of the Son of God amongst His people. It must always be characterized by the place and prominence it gives to the person, office and work of our matchless Saviour.

The early disciples had been with Jesus and the outside world could not fail to recognize it. Their lives were Christ-captured, Christ-centered and Christ-controlled. In his writings Luke says, ". . . when they saw the boldness of Peter and John, and perceived that they were unlearned and ignorant men, they marvelled; and they took knowledge of them, that they had been with Jesus" (vs. 13). The Apostle Paul writes of the same experience when he declares, "For to me to live [or, life itself] is Christ . . ." (Philippians 1:21). Thus where-ever the apostles went, and whatever they said or did, Christ was seen and heard and felt.

The Lord Jesus Christ always creates an issue. That was true of His human life on earth. Study His contact with individuals, groups or even multitudes, and you will notice that He never neutralizes. He always antagonized or attracted them. When He spoke people either believed on Him or they picked up stones to stone Him. In the Gospel of John particularly, we come across words like this: "There was a division therefore again among the Jews for these sayings. And many of them said, He hath a devil, and is mad; why hear ye him? Others said, These are not the words of him that hath a devil.

Can a devil open the eyes of the blind?" (John 10:19-21) We must never forget that He is the same Lord who indwells us by the power of the Holy Spirit and the same decisiveness of living and influence should characterize the Christ-centered, Christ-controlled life.

Yes, the disciples had been with Jesus. In other words, He was *the subject of their confession.* ". . . when they saw the boldness of Peter and John . . ." (vs. 13). The word "boldness" suggests the idea of fluency and freedom of speech. In other words, their confession was fearless. Dr. William Barclay says, "When we read the speech of Peter, we must remember to whom it was spoken, and when we do remember that, it becomes one of the world's great demonstrations of courage. It was spoken to an audience of the wealthiest, the most intellectual and the most powerful in the land, and yet Peter, the Galilean fisherman, stands before them rather as their judge than as their victim. But further, this was the very crowd which had condemned Jesus to death. Peter knew it, and he knew that at this moment he was taking his life in his hands. There are two kinds of courage. There is the reckless courage which goes on scarce aware of the dangers it is facing. There is the far higher, cool, calculated courage which knows the peril in which it stands and which will not be daunted. It was that second courage that Peter demonstrated to men. When Achilles, the great warrior of the Greeks, was told that if he went out to battle he would surely die, he answered in the immortal sentence, 'Nevertheless, I am for going on.' Peter, in that moment, knew the peril in which he stood; nevertheless, he, too, was for going on."

With that vivid description of the context and climate of that immortal occasion, listen again to the fearless words that issue from Peter's lips: "Then Peter, filled with the Holy Ghost, said unto them, Ye rulers of the people, and elders of Israel, If we this day be examined of the good deed done to the impotent man, by what means he is made whole; Be it known unto you all, and to all the people of Israel, that by the name of Jesus Christ of Nazareth, *whom ye crucified,* whom God raised from the dead, even by him doth this man stand here before you whole" (vss. 8-10). Did you ever read of such fearlessness? And remember, this is the man who crouched and cringed at the sneer of a servant girl who accused him of being associated with Jesus on that fateful night before the crucifixion.

But something has happened to this man. He is full of the Holy Ghost and with that fullness comes a truly remarkable freedom and fearlessness of confession. This is why revival spread—this is why those men left a spiritual wake behind them wherever they went or preached. It was a fearless confession, but it was also a faithful confession. It summed up everything. Peter could say, "This is the stone which was set at nought of you builders, which is become the head of the corner. Neither is there salvation in any other: for there is none other name under heaven given among men, whereby we must be saved" (vss. 11-12).

You cannot imagine anything more faithful. Peter was narrowing the salvation of God right down to one gospel, one name, one Person—even the Lord Jesus. There is no sense of embarrassment; no apology for dragging religion into his address. There is no attempt at rationalizing the plain and simple fact that Jesus is the only Saviour of men. And do not forget, all this was spoken to the very same members of the Sanhedrin who had condemned Jesus to death fifty days earlier.

Consider further not only the subject of their confession, but *the strength of their conviction.* "Now when they saw the boldness of Peter and John, and perceived that they were unlearned and ignorant men, they marvelled . . ." (vs. 13). Christians have always been attacked along the lines of intellectualism and professionalism, but God has always had His answer through His chosen instruments. Even Paul recognizes this when he says, ". . . ye see your calling, brethren, how that not many wise men after the flesh, not many mighty, not many noble, are called: But God hath chosen the foolish things of the world to confound the wise; and God hath chosen the weak things of the world . . . and things which are despised, hath God chosen, yea, and things which are not, to bring to nought things which are: That no flesh should glory . . ." (I Corinthians 1:26-29).

So God took Peter, and John completely identified with him, to confound the intellectuals and professionals of his day. Let us not be unmindful, however, of the fact that though ordinary fishermen, they had been under the discipline, example and instruction of the greatest Teacher the world has ever known, even the Master Himself. But notwithstanding, carnal intellectualism and professionalism will still find fault. Think of what the religious leaders said of Jesus Himself when they asked, "How knoweth this man letters, having never learned?" (John 7:15). And remember what the carnal Corinthians had to say about the Apostle Paul: "For his letters . . . are weighty and powerful; but his bodily presence is weak, and his speech contemptible" (II Corinthians 10:10). And here again, the Jews having ". . . perceived [or, having ascertained] that they were unlearned and ignorant men, they marvelled . . ." (vs. 13).

Bishop Charles John Ellicott points out that "the first of the two words means, literally, unlettered. Looking to the special meaning of the 'letters' of 'Scriptures' of the Jews, from which the scribes took their name (*grammateis*, from *grammata*), it would convey, as used here the sense of 'not having been educated as a scribe, not having studied the Law and other sacred writings.' This word does not occur elsewhere in the New Testament. The second word means, literally, a private person, one without special office or calling or the culture which they imply: what in English might be called a 'common man.'" The Bishop goes on to state that later this word acquired the sense of "an idiot."

In a word, the criticism of Peter and John is that they were neither intellectual nor professional. "But hasn't that always been the story?" says Master Trappe, quoting Tertullian. In the days of the early church the world caricatured the God of the Christian with an ass's head and a book in His hand because they maintained it was a religion without learning. The

Jesuit priests condemned the Puritans alleging that they were "a lot of blockheads." But notwithstanding all this hostile reaction there was no gainsaying the strength of conviction that came through the lives and lips of these Spirit-anointed revivalists, a conviction so characterized by irresistible wisdom that even the intellectuals and professionals had to "marvel."

Jesus was the subject of their confession, the strength of their conviction, but also *the substance of their communion.* ". . . they took knowledge of them, that they had been with Jesus" (vs. 13). Jesus was the center and secret of an indivisible fellowship. He was the point of integration for their common life, love and loyalty.

These then were the secrets of the spreading revival, and in the wake of this spiritual movement thousands were turning to Christ and Christianity, which was a factor to be reckoned with.

But a second question arises:

II WHAT ARE THE SIGNS OF SPREADING REVIVAL?

The chapter before us and indeed the whole of the Acts of the Apostles are full of such signs, but they may be summed up thus: *the miraculous events.* The astounded enemies of Christ had to ask, "What shall we do to these men? for that indeed a notable miracle hath been done by them is manifest to all them that dwell in Jerusalem; and we cannot deny it" (vs. 16). Revival has always been accompanied by miraculous events, because it is the function of the Holy Spirit to effect miracles. And let us not overlook the fact that we are still living in the age of the Spirit. Pentecost was not just a day; it was a dispensation or the age of the church. God forgive us for having narrowed down the operation of the Holy Spirit to our theological systems, our traditional forms, our denominational organizations and, worst of all, our deplorable unbelief. It has yet to be seen in our day what God can accomplish when men and women truly say and mean, "I believe in the

Holy Ghost." Then, and only then, shall we see miraculous events taking place through the ministry of praying, preaching and healing.

Another sign was *the conspicuous effects.* "So when they had further threatened them, they let them go, finding nothing how they might punish them, because of the people: for all men glorified God for that which was done" (vs. 21). As we have already observed, thousands had been converted already and God was continuing to save daily such as should be saved. Furthermore, healings were taking place, and the whole city was being impacted by the power of the gospel so that all men glorified God for that which was done. Nothing was happening in a corner. Everybody was aware of the fact that Jesus was alive, that His name symbolized a life-transforming gospel, and that His followers were fearless and unchallengeable witnesses to a new spiritual movement. True, there was opposition, as we have seen only too clearly, but that also is a conspicuous effect of revival.

So there were the miraculous events, the conspicuous effects, and also *the victorious exploits.* I thrill again and again as I read the language of Peter and John as they stand arraigned before the Sanhedrin: "Whether it be right in the sight of God to hearken unto you more than unto God, judge ye. For we cannot but speak the things which we have seen and heard" (vss. 19-20). Here were men who knew that they were on the victory side and nothing was going to hold them back. I can almost hear them saying one to another, "By the power of the Holy Spirit we have taken the metropolis of Jerusalem; now let us go on to the next city." It is a question of moving forward to greater and yet greater exploits for God, and in the wake of the great revival they left behind them innumerable men and women and boys and girls who had entered into life.

How that contrasts with the pessimism and defeatism of today. We hear it all around us by the people who say that this could never happen again. And because of our unbelief even the Son of God Himself can do no mighty miracles. We have so relegated God to a secondary place and grieved the Holy

Spirit by organizational, promotional and drumbeating activities, that we have lost the victorious outlook that follows in the train of the Saviour's triumph. O that God would turn again our captivity until we see the signs of spreading revival once again!

But there is a further question which must detain us. It is:

III WHAT IS THE SCOPE OF SPREADING REVIVAL?

In the light of the teaching of the Book of the Acts, we can sum up the scope of spreading revival in the one phrase, "the life of the Spirit." Wherever we look we find expressions which will convince even the casual reader that these early Christians were not only filled with the Spirit, but lived in the Spirit and fellowshiped in the Spirit. In other words, they knew *the fullness of the Spirit.* "And when they had prayed, the place was shaken where they were assembled together; and they were all filled with the Holy Ghost . . ." (vs. 31). It is repetitious but essential to state once again that there can be no revival outside of the fullness of the Holy Spirit. Only within the scope of this spiritual fullness can there be ". . . times of refreshing . . . from the presence of the Lord" (Acts 3:19). The question we must ask ourselves continually is, "Am I consciously, believingly, victoriously full of the Holy Ghost?" It was because Peter was full of the Holy Ghost that he could preach for God (4:8); it was because Stephen was full of the Holy Ghost that he could suffer for God (7:55); it was because Barnabas was full of the Holy Ghost that he could exhort for God (11:24); it was because Saul, who became Paul, was full of the Holy Ghost that he could rebuke for God (13:9); and so it goes right through the Acts of the Apostles.

This scope of spreading revival might also be described as *the freedom of the Spirit.* ". . . they were all filled with the Holy Ghost, and they spake the word of God with boldness" (4:31). Earlier in our study we noticed that this word "boldness" suggests freedom, fluency and fearlessness. But let us remember that liberty does not suggest the desire to do what you want. Liberty is rather the power to do what you ought. To put it another way, liberty is not license. Therefore, the freedom of the Holy Spirit will never lead to unhealthy extremism or anything else that would dishonor the person of our Lord Jesus Christ. The freedom of the Holy Spirit is a spiritual control which constrains and restrains the individual believer or a group of believers within the will of God.

Another aspect of the scope of spreading revival was *the fellowship of the Spirit.* "And the multitude of them that believed were of one heart and of one soul: neither said any of them that ought of the things which he possessed was his own; but they had all things common" (4:32). Here was a movement of the Spirit within the whole true church of Christ. This was no splinter group activity. On the contrary, all who believed were of one heart and of one soul. If you like, it was a kind of Christian communism in which everything was shared: ". . . neither said any of them that ought of the things which he possessed was his own. . . ." The life and gifts and service of Christ were shared together. This was genuine participation or communion.

Here we have the scope of true revival—the fullness, freedom and fellowship of the Spirit. No wonder things were happening in the wake of this mighty spiritual movement. "Can it happen again?" you ask. The answer is, "Positively yes," for the Holy Spirit is as powerful today as He was on the day of Pentecost. All He waits for is the church, made up of men and women who are prepared to quit grieving Him and quenching Him in order that He might fill and overflow in revival blessing to life's remotest point.

The serious problem of our age is that Christian men and women are sinning against the Holy Ghost. The Puritan, John Calvin, was right, and John Owen who quotes him confirms the fact that the sin of Old Testament times was the rejection of Jehovah God, the sin of New Testament times was the rejection of the Son of God, and the sin of the church age is the rejection of the Holy Spirit. There are so-called believers all over Christendom today who refuse to acknowledge the sovereignty of the Holy Spirit within the church, as well as within the individual life. These people are not living in the fullness and freedom and fellowship of the Spirit. This is why we do not know a contagious revival. But let us not be pessimistic; revival can come and will come carrying in its wake all the blessings which are promised to us in Christ, if we are prepared to discover the secret, discern the signs and determine the scope of a heaven-sent spiritual revival.

Let us then start to pray for this in the language of Charles H. Gabriel:

> Lord, as of old at Pentecost
> Thou didst Thy power display,
> With cleansing, purifying flame
> Descend on us today.
>
> For mighty works for Thee, prepare
> And strengthen every heart;
> Come, take possession of Thine own,
> And nevermore depart.
>
> All self consume, all sin destroy!
> With earnest zeal endue
> Each waiting heart to work for Thee;
> O Lord, our faith renew!
>
> Speak, Lord! before Thy throne we wait,
> Thy promise we believe,
> And will not let Thee go until
> The blessing we receive.

Be patient therefore, brethren, unto the coming of the Lord. Behold, the husbandman waiteth for the precious fruit of the earth, and hath long patience for it, until he receive the early and latter rain.
Be ye also patient; stablish your hearts: for the coming of the Lord draweth nigh.
Grudge not one against another, brethren, lest ye be condemned: behold, the judge standeth before the door.
Take, my brethren, the prophets, who have spoken in the name of the Lord, for an example of suffering affliction, and of patience.
Behold, we count them happy which endure. Ye have heard of the patience of Job, and have seen the end of the Lord; that the Lord is very pitiful, and of tender mercy.

JAMES 5:7-11

8
The "WAIT" of Revival

A GREEK CHURCH FATHER KNOWN AS CLEMENT, BORN ABOUT A.D. 150, informs us that James and his brother Jude were farmers. That explains why James so often uses vivid illustrations from a farmer's life. He speaks, for instance, in the verses before us, of the rain of seedtime, and the rain of ripening harvest. The first fell in Judea about the middle of October, after the seed was sown, and the second towards the end of April, when the ears were filling and ripening for harvest. Without those two rains the earth would have been unfruitful.

What a glorious illustration this is of the final harvest before the heavenly Husbandman returns for the precious fruit of the earth. The fact that "the latter rain" is yet to fall gives me great confidence in believing that the church is yet to witness revival—even though concurrently with it the world will grow more wicked, defiant and meet for divine judgment.

The "latter rain" of revival suggests:

I THE PROMISE OF GOD IN RELATION TO REVIVAL

". . . the husbandman . . . hath long patience . . . until he receive the early and latter rain" (vs. 7). It is both interesting and instructive to observe that God has promised the "early and latter rain" in terms of *physical fulfillment*. When the children of Israel were about to enter the land of Canaan, God said through Moses: ". . . I will give you the rain of your land in his due season, the first rain and the latter rain, that thou mayest gather in thy corn, and thy wine, and thine oil" (Deuteronomy 11:11-14). It is quite clear from this passage, and a number of others, that the harvest was dependent upon the rain, and that the rain was promised by God, contingent upon obedience. When the nation followed God, there was rain, harvest and plenty. On the other hand, when there was a departure from the way of righteousness, then there was drought, famine and distress. We are all familiar with the story of Elijah who was commanded to pray that it might not rain, and we read in the very chapter before us: ". . . it rained not on the earth by the space of three years and six months. And he prayed again, and the heaven gave rain, and the earth brought forth her fruit" (James 5:17-18). Thus God taught His people that His purpose for them was "the early and latter rain"—if only they would be obedient to His Word.

But what had been true in the physical life of God's ancient people had been equally true in the spiritual life of all His people, Jew and Gentile. The promise of "early and latter rain" has a *spiritual fulfillment*. "Behold, the husbandman waiteth . . . until he receive the early and latter rain" (vs. 7). During Old Testament times the rain of revival fell again and again at such periods of spiritual awakening and renewal as are indicated throughout the history of the Jews. But when we come to the New Testament, it can be clearly shown that Pentecost was the historical and spiritual commencement of the fall of the "early rain." Indeed, such was the outpouring of the Holy Spirit in those days that in little more than thirty years the whole of the civilized world was evangelized for Christ and the ground prepared for the final harvest.

Since then the rain of blessing has not entirely ceased. Like the occasional showers that continue to fall from October through to the latter rain of April, in Palestine, there have been notable downpours of revival throughout the history of the church. Particularly has it been so since the Reformation. But now we await the final outpouring, "the latter rain." It is quite evident from our text that this is going to precede the coming of the Lord and, therefore, coincide with the final harvest. The Lord Jesus explained in the parable of the tares that

". . . the harvest is the end of the world . . ." (Matthew 13: 39-41). And then He will come with His sickle to reap the precious fruit of the earth. (See Revelation 14:14-16.)

If this be so, then before our Saviour returns we must expect the promised rain of harvest. O that it might begin to fall soon! If we believe that God's promise concerning the second advent of His Son must and will be fulfilled, we must also believe that He will honor His promise concerning "the latter rain" of revival.

In the second place, I want you to notice that "the latter rain" of revival suggests:

II THE PURPOSE OF GOD IN RELATION TO REVIVAL

"Behold, the husbandman waiteth for the precious fruit of the earth, and hath long patience for it. . . . Be ye also patient; . . . for the coming of the Lord draweth nigh" (vss. 7-8). The purpose of God in relation to revival is twofold: first, *to hasten the day of harvest.* ". . . the husbandman waiteth for the precious fruit of the earth . . ." (vs. 7). The Holy Scriptures and the story of revivals show that the greatest harvesting periods in history have been always characterized by the outpouring of the Holy Spirit. That there is a great harvest to reap is beyond dispute. The Master in His day said, "The harvest truly is plenteous, but the labourers are few; Pray ye therefore the Lord of the harvest, that he will send forth labourers into his harvest" (Matthew 9:37-38). And again: "Say not ye, There are yet four months, and then cometh harvest? behold, I say unto you, Lift up your eyes, and look on the fields; for they are white already to harvest" (John 4:35).

If these words carried a sense of urgency about them nearly two thousand years ago, what about today—with the shrinkage of the globe, the explosion of population, and the advanced media of communicating the gospel? The only lack, and vital lack, is the pouring out of the Spirit in revival. All our efforts, otherwise, however modern, scientific and advanced, are worthless.

God's purpose in revival is to hasten the day of harvest and also *to hasten the day of heaven.* ". . . for the coming of the Lord draweth nigh" (vs. 8). The Apostle Peter expresses the same thought when he exhorts believers to "Look for and hasten the coming of the day of God" (II Peter 3:12, marginal rendering).

It is one of the functions of the Holy Spirit in the believer to make him homesick for heaven. Paul puts it this way: "But we all, with open face beholding as in a glass the glory of the Lord, are changed into the same image from glory to glory, even as by the Spirit of the Lord" (II Corinthians 3:18). The more the Holy Spirit fills and transforms us, the more we become like Jesus and are fitted for heaven.

If the early rain is necessary for the germination of the seed, the latter rain is needful for the fructification of the same. If the church would only experience a season of revival, we would see transforming changes take place with amazing rapidity.

One more thought suggested by the "latter rain" is that of:

III THE PATIENCE OF GOD IN RELATION TO REVIVAL

"Be patient therefore, brethren, unto the coming of the Lord. Behold, the husbandman waiteth for the precious fruit of the earth, and hath long patience for it. . . . Be ye also patient; stablish your hearts: for the coming of the Lord draweth nigh" (vss. 7-8). The quality of patience is a divine virtue. The word signifies long-suffering and suggests brave endurance of afflictions and the refusal to give way under them, even under pressure. Patience is that holy self-restraint which enables the sufferer to refrain from hasty retaliation. Patience has nothing whatsoever to do with indifference, apathy or stoicism. Since God has promised and purposed revival, He patiently waits for it, regardless of circumstances in the world and conditions in the church. In like manner the believer is to exercise patience. In fact, where there is no patience in relation to revival, there is no prayer for revival, and therefore no faith in God's promise and purpose in revival. So James draws attention to the patience of God in order that the believer might do two things: the first is to *emulate extended patience.* "Be ye also patient; stablish your hearts: for the coming of the Lord draweth nigh" (vs. 8). God is patient; the Lord Jesus is patient; the Holy Spirit is patient; the prophets of old were patient. Concerning the latter, James says, "Take, my brethren, the prophets, who have spoken in the name of the Lord, for an example of suffering affliction, and of patience. Behold, we count them happy which endure. Ye have heard of the patience of Job, and have seen the end of the Lord; that the Lord is very pitiful, and of tender mercy" (vss. 10-11).

There is hardly a prophet in the Old Testament who could not be shown to be in some way an "example of suffering affliction, and of patience." Stephen, in his defense before the religious leaders of his day, asked his accusers this question: "Which of the prophets have not your fathers persecuted?" (Acts 7:52).

Jesus said: "Blessed are ye, when men shall revile you, and persecute you, and shall say all manner of evil against you falsely, for my sake. Rejoice, and be exceeding glad: for great is your reward in heaven: for so persecuted they the prophets which were before you" (Matthew 5:11-12).

Perhaps the prophet that James had in mind, above all others, was Jeremiah—who later became known as *the* prophet. Professor R. V. G. Tasker says of him: "This hypersensitive, warmhearted patriot, compelled to proclaim a succession of divine messages to his countrymen that were unpopular because they were of necessity pessimistic, who was so sympathetic towards the sufferings of others, was himself beaten, put in the stocks, imprisoned in a dungeon, and thrown into a cistern by the very men whom he would gladly have saved if such salvation had been possible, from the doom that awaited them. His life was one of almost perpetual physical and spiritual suffering, yet his demeanor throughout was such that, of all the historical characters of the Old Testament, he was the one who most foreshadowed Him Who, when He was reviled, reviled not again, and Who suffered for man's salvation the physical and spiritual agony of the cross."

Then, of course, James mentions Job in verse 11. The word "patience" used of him is not the same as the word employed in the previous verses. It is a term which implies "constancy and endurance." "No English word," writes F. J. A. Hort, "is quite strong enough to express the active courage and resolution here implied."

What a familiar story is Job's record of constancy, endurance, and steadfastness! To quote Professor Tasker once again:

It is not so much the self-restraint of Job under affliction, leading him to be patient with others, that is here emphasized, for Job was very far from showing patience in this sense with his so-called comforters. What Job did, however, display in a marked degree was the determination to endure whatever might fall to his lot without losing faith in God. He believed even when he could not understand.

When blow after blow had fallen upon him in rapid succession Job cried, "Naked came I out of my mother's womb, and naked shall I return thither: the Lord gave, and the Lord hath taken away; blessed be the name of the Lord" (Job 1:21). His reply to his wife when she invited him to curse God and die was, "Thou speakest as one of the foolish women speaketh. What? shall we receive good at the hand of God, and shall we not receive evil?" (Job 2:10). To "the physicians of no value" who posed as his friends, his answer was, "Though he slay me, yet will I trust in him" (13:15). He was convinced that his witness was in heaven and his record with the most high (16:19); and he knew that his Redeemer was alive (19:25).

The end of the Lord was the complete vindication of Job by his Maker. Not only were his material possessions and his worldly prosperity restored to him, but he was granted a fuller understanding of the mystery of the divine purpose, and a more direct experience of the majesty and sovereignty of Almighty God; and he became capable of a greater and deeper penitence. "I have heard of thee by the hearing of the ear," he was able to cry, "but now mine eye seeth thee: Wherefore I abhor myself, and repent in dust and ashes" (42:5-6). So it was that "the Lord blessed the latter end of Job more than his beginning" (42:12). The God, whose severity Job had for so long experienced, as his character was tested in the furnace of affliction, in the end showed Himself to be, in the words of the Psalmist quoted by James, *very pitiful, and of tender mercy* (Psa. 103:8).

What a call to patience this is! But before we move from this point, however, it is important that we should note the manner in which we are to emulate extended patience. James exhorts, "Be ye also patient; stablish your hearts: for the coming of the Lord draweth nigh" (vs. 8).

The twofold secret of maintained patience is intercession and expectation. The word for "stablish" in the Septuagint is the same as that which is used for the bolstering or holding up of Moses' hands (Exodus 17:12). Patience for revival can only be bolstered up by prayer. Then there is the spirit of expectation which should characterize every truly born-again soul. For the Apostle Peter reminds us that we are begotten . . . unto a living hope (I Peter 1:3). If we have the hope and believe God's promise, we cannot but patiently await the glorious fulfillments of revival and the coming again of the Lord Jesus Christ.

So we are to emulate extended patience—as seen in God Himself and as reproduced in the saints who have left us an ". . . example of suffering affliction, and of patience" (vs. 10). But the patience of God is also designed to *deprecate exhausted patience.* "Grudge not one against another, brethren, lest ye be condemned: behold, the judge standeth before the door" (vs. 9).

The word "grudge" means to "grumble, murmur, or complain." Under the pressure of opposition, persecution and tribulation we can soon exhaust our patience—unless we are drawing heavily on the resources of God. At such times as these we fall victims to the sin and spirit of grumbling, murmuring, and complaining. We blame God for not answering our prayers for revival, and then we criticize one another for being hindrances to blessing, without recognizing all the while that we are under condemnation ourselves. The Word says that to grumble is to be condemned. Let us never forget that ". . . the judge standeth before the door" (vs. 9). He hears and knows everything; and when He comes He will judge everything. "For we must all appear before the judgment seat of Christ; that every one may receive the things done in his body, according to that he hath done, whether it be good or bad" (II Corinthians 5:10).

Let us see to it then that we never exhaust our patience and become a grumbling people. For unbelief and grumbling the children of Israel were all barred (save two men) from the promised land of blessing. It is possible to be by-passed by revival even when it comes. God save us from such a tragedy!

So we have observed that "the latter rain" of revival suggests to us the promise, purpose and patience of God in relation to revival. O that we might be given the patience for the latter rain of revival which made John Newton write:

Saviour, visit Thy plantation,
  Grant us, Lord, a gracious rain!
All will come to desolation,
  Unless Thou return again.
Keep no longer at a distance,
  Shine upon us from on high,
Lest, for want of Thine assistance,
  Every plant should droop and die.

Surely once Thy garden flourish'd!
  Every part look'd gay and green;
Then Thy Word our spirits nourish'd;
  Happy seasons we have seen!
But a drought has since succeeded,
  And a sad decline we see;
Lord, Thy help is greatly needed,
  Help can only come from Thee!

Where are those we counted leaders,
  Fill'd with zeal and love and truth—
Old professors, tall as cedars,

Bright examples of our youth?
Some, in whom we once delighted,
We shall meet no more below;
Some, alas! we fear are blighted.
Scarce a single leaf they show.

Younger plants—the sight how pleasant!—
Cover'd thick with blossoms stood;
But they cause us grief at present,
Frosts have nipp'd them in the bud!
Dearest Saviour, hasten hither;
Thou canst make them bloom again;
Oh, permit them not to wither,
Let not all our hopes be vain!

Let our mutual love be fervent,
Make us prevalent in prayers;
Let each one esteem'd Thy servant
Shun the world's bewitching snares.
Break the tempter's fatal power,
Turn the stony heart to flesh;
And begin, from this good hour,
To revive Thy work afresh.

CONCLUSION

As was stated at the beginning, the aim of these chapters has been to spell out a "Heart-Cry for Revival" in terms of biblical teaching and in the context of contemporary need. For the purpose of this book, that task is now completed. All that remains is to illustrate what has been said with some stories of what will happen when we *believe* God to send revival. The examples I have chosen cover the areas of the personal life, the local church, and the mission field.

Perhaps the most vivid recollection I have of revival in the personal life is the story of Evan Roberts, the leader of the Welsh revival of 1904-5. I had the privilege of meeting him personally, not long before he died, in the city of Cardiff, South Wales. What he said to me in that brief but meaningful interview will always live with me. Although he was well nigh seventy years of age and rather feeble in body, it was evident to any discerning spirit that here was a man who knew the God of revival. It is no wonder that, when he died on January 29, 1951, in a little nursing home in Cardiff, at the age of seventy-two, the British paper, called the *News Chronicle*, wrote that "Wales mourns her greatest prophet."

Evan Roberts was born at Loughor in 1878 and, after a period as miner and blacksmith, he entered the grammar school at Newcastle-Emlyn in preparation for the Christian ministry. Even in those days, God was beginning to stir in his young heart, giving him an insatiable hunger for heaven-sent revival. Indeed it was while he was at this school that he attended a conference at a place called Blaenanerch, in September 1904. Those meetings were convened to consider the spiritual life of the churches in the area and to decide on what action to take. It was during the conference that Evan Roberts was "filled with the Holy Ghost."

"For thirteen years," writes Evan Roberts, "I had prayed for the Spirit; and this is the way I was led to pray. William Davies, the deacon, said one night in the society: 'Remember to be faithful. What if the Spirit descended and you were absent? Remember Thomas! What a loss he had.'

"I said to myself: 'I will have the Spirit'; and through every kind of weather and in spite of all difficulties, I went to the meetings. Many times, on seeing other boys with the boats on the tide, I was tempted to turn back and join them. But, no. I said to myself: 'Remember your resolve,' and on I went. I went faithfully to the meetings for prayer throughout the ten or eleven years I prayed for a Revival. It was the Spirit that moved me thus to think."

At a certain morning meeting which Evan Roberts attended, the evangelist in one of his petitions besought that the Lord would "bend us." The Spirit seemed to say to Roberts, "That's what you need, to be bent." And thus he describes his experience: "I felt a living force coming into my bosom. This grew and grew, and I was almost bursting. My bosom was boiling. What boiled in me was that verse: 'God commending His love.' I fell on my knees with my arms over the seat in front of me; the tears and perspiration flowed freely. I thought blood was gushing forth." Certain friends approached to wipe his face. Meanwhile he was crying out, "O Lord, bend me! Bend me!" Then suddenly the glory broke.

Mr. Roberts adds: "After I was bent, a wave of peace came over me, and the audience sang, 'I hear Thy welcome voice.' And as they sang I thought about the bending at the Judgment Day, and I was filled with compassion for those that would have to bend on that day, and I wept.

"Henceforth, the salvation of souls became the burden of my heart. From that time I was on fire with a desire to go through all Wales, and if it were possible, I was willing to pray God for the privilege of going."

From that point onward, this young man of twenty-six went

everywhere spreading the fires of revival. The chapels were thronged, with hundreds more outside. His appearance at these gatherings often caused much religious fervor and excitement, and a few words of exhortation or a brief prayer sufficed to set the congregation ablaze. The people would burst into singing and then testimony, followed by prayer, and then into singing again. Indeed, it is said that all Wales seemed like a praise meeting. Mealtimes and other routine practices were neglected and forgotten, and God moved throughout the whole principality in saving and purifying power. Heaven-sent revival had truly visited Wales.

And the point of the story is that it all started with a man who was prepared to pray, "O Lord, bend me! Bend me!" Can this happen today? I most certainly believe it can.

What can happen in the area of the personal life can also take place in a local church. To illustrate this, I want to quote quite extensively from the story of the Reverend Joseph Kemp, as told by his wife.

Joseph Kemp was an orphan whom God took up and gloriously saved in the 1880's, and prepared as a vessel unto honor, meet for the Master's use. After some training at the Bible Institute of Glasgow, Mr. Kemp was led into small pastorates and then finally to the now well-known Charlotte Chapel of Edinburgh. After a most fruitful ministry in that city, he came over to the United States to become the minister of Calvary Baptist Church, New York City. Subsequently, he went to New Zealand, where he led the work at the Auckland Baptist Tabernacle. During his closing years, he founded the New Zealand Bible Institute and was greatly used in bringing blessing and revival to churches, as well as to individual lives, throughout the whole of that land.

My main concern, however, is what happened at Charlotte Chapel under his God-anointed ministry. And here let me refer directly to his biography:

> Soon after the Welsh revival broke out, I went to Wales, where I spent two weeks watching, experiencing, drinking in, having my own heart searched, comparing my methods with those of the Holy

Ghost; and then I returned to my people in Edinburgh to tell what I had seen. In Wales I saw the people had learned to sing in a way which to me was new. I never heard such singing as theirs. They sang such old familiar hymns as "When I survey the wondrous Cross," and "There is a fountain filled with Blood," and "I need Thee, oh, I need Thee." They needed no organist or choir or leader. Their singing was natural. The Holy Ghost was in their singing as much as in any other exercise. They had the New Song. People tell us our religion is joyless. Well, if the saints of the Living God have no joy, who has? Jesus Christ has given us to see that joy is one of the qualities He imparts to the saints of God. The world knows nothing of it. Do not tell me that the sporting clubs, the dance halls, the movies, and operas can give you joy. They can for the moment give you some fun, but that is not joy. Joy is the gift of God. When a revival from God visits a congregation it brings with it joy.

The dominating note of the Welsh revival was redemption through the Blood. There, too, was the recognition of the Lordship of Christ. It is the same old story from age to age. There is no new way of bringing men to Christ. There must be the recognition of sin, and the joyful recognition that sin can be blotted out by the Blood of the Lamb, and a Blood-washed soul kept and sanctified by the Lord Jesus Christ.

The evening he returned from Wales was memorable. A large meeting was in full swing when he walked down the aisle of the chapel. The people listened eagerly as he told of his visit and its effect upon his own soul. After telling the story he tested the meeting, asking if there was a man willing to be saved. About five seats from the front a man rose, saying, "I want you to pray for me." This man was the first of hundreds who were saved during the revival in Charlotte Chapel.

The people were now on the tiptoe of expectancy for a revival. A Conference on January 22, 1906, addressed by several workers who had visited Wales, lasted from 3:30 P.M. until midnight. From that day it was felt that the fire of God had fallen; and as far as Charlotte Chapel was concerned, God had answered prayer and reviving had come. By the end of 1905, the church had been praying one whole year without so much as one solitary break. Night after night, week after week, month after month, the prayer meetings went on increasing in numbers and intensity. It is impossible to convey any adequate idea of the prayer passion that characterized those meetings. There was little or no preaching, it being no uncommon experience for the pastor to go to the pulpit on the Lord's Day, and find the congregation so caught in the spirit of prayer as to render preaching out of the question.

The people poured out their hearts in importunate prayer. I have yet to witness a movement that has produced more permanent results in the lives of men, women, and children. There were irregularities, no doubt; some commotion, yes. There was that which shot itself through all prescribed forms and shattered all conventionality. But such a movement with all its irregularities is to be preferred far above the dull, dreary, monotonous decorum of many churches. Under these influences the crowds thronged the chapel, which only three years before maintained a "sombre vacuum." After the first year of this work we had personally dealt with no fewer than one thousand souls, who had been brought to God during the prayer meetings.

"It is impossible to record in detail the striking incidents of the revival movement of 1905," Mr. Kemp wrote. "If its genuineness can be attested by its results, then we need have no doubt regarding it. It has given us a full church night and morning, which of itself is something to be profoundly thankful for in days when it is conceded the churches have lost their hold on the people. It has given us a most loyal and devoted band of workers, whose aim is the glory of God in the salvation of sinners. It has taught us to pray in a fashion few of us knew of before. It has given to both young and old a new love for the Bible. Time would fail to tell of the purified lives, changed homes, and the brightened outlook of hundreds."

In 1906 the movement seemed to have found its level, and arrangements were made to reorganize the work on generally accepted Church lines. But again the revival fires blazed forth, and the meetings became marked by a deeper outgoing of the soul to God in prayer than ever; and a passionately expressed desire for the salvation of men was a dominant feature. Towards the close of 1906 there were indications that the Lord was about to move in our midst once more. The attendances at the 7 A.M. prayer meetings on Lord's Days increased, and the meetings were marked by a deepening spirit of prayer. This was followed up by the same prayer spirit in the week-night meetings.

"On Saturday, December 20, our monthly conference and evening meeting were addressed by friends who had previously experienced a quickening in their own souls: and their testimony, given in the power of the Holy Ghost, awakened longings in the hearts of many for Revival. One and another, some secretly, some publicly, claimed Divine anointing for service. Some went home that Saturday night, but could not sleep. One brother told the next day how the deep conviction that the Revival so long prayed for was at hand, had kept him awake for the most part of the night. A singular and remarkable thing is, that many who were not present at these meetings had at the same time the impression borne in on them that the Lord was about to work.

"The meetings on Lord's Day were marked by an earnest outgoing of the soul to God in prayer, and a passionately expressed desire for the salvation of men, all of which told of the dealings many had had—Jacob-like—with God alone. It was, however, at a late prayer meeting, held in the evening at 9:30, that the fire of God fell. There was nothing, humanly speaking, to account for what happened. Quite suddenly, upon one and another came an overwhelming sense of the reality and awfulness of His presence and of eternal things. Life, death, and eternity seemed suddenly laid bare. Prayer and weeping began, and gained in intensity every moment. As on the day of laying the foundation of the second temple, 'the people could not discern the noise of the shout of joy from the noise of the weeping of the people' (Erza iii. 13). One was overwhelmed before the sudden bursting of the bounds. Could it be real? We looked up and asked for clear directions, and all we knew of guidance was, 'Do nothing.' Friends who were gathered sang on their knees. Each seemed to sing, and each seemed to pray, oblivious of one another.

"Then the prayer broke out again, waves and waves of prayer; and the midnight hour was reached. The hours had passed like minutes. It is useless being a spectator looking on, or praying for it, in order to catch its spirit and breath. It is necessary to be in it, praying in it, part of it, caught by the same power, swept by the same wind. One who was present says: 'I cannot tell you what Christ was to me last night. My heart was full to overflowing. If ever my Lord was near to me, it was last night.'

"Our programme drawn up for the watchnight service and New Year's Day had to give way before this Divine visitation. Early on the last night of the old year, friends gathered for prayer, and continued until the beginning of the watchnight service at 10:30, at which meeting the power of the Lord was again manifest. What the closing hours of 1906 meant to many, only the Eternal Day will reveal. Crushed, broken, and penitent on account of the defeated past, many of us again knelt at the Cross; and as the bells rang in the New Year, we vowed by God's grace to press into our lives more service for Him, to be more like Him in spirit and walk, and win to Him our fellow-men.

"The Chapel was opened all day on the 1st of January, and meetings were held at 11, 3, and 6:30. At every meeting, especially in the afternoon and evening, God drew near. The afternoon meeting got entirely beyond a cut-and-dried programme, and resolved itself into one of prayer, confession, testimony, and praise. Testimonies from friends at home and visitors from a distance were given to the fresh power which had come into their lives. The evening meeting went on without the guidance of any human hand; and though friends were present who had been engaged to address it, no address could be given. The people were bowed in prayer, heart-searching, and contrition. And it was only while thus waiting that light broke in upon many hearts, once more revealing and bringing to light the 'hidden things of darkness' and compelling separation from sin unto God. During the meetings a number of unconverted persons decided for Christ; but the burden of all the meetings was that 'judgment must begin at the house of God.'

"Meetings of a similar character have been going on for over a fortnight. To the curious the meetings appear disorderly; but to those who are in them and of them, there is order in the midst of disorder. The confusion never gets confused; the meetings are held by invisible Hands. Believers have been awakened to a sense of having lived defeated lives, bound by the 'law of sin and death'; progress retarded by 'weights' and 'sins'; spiritual growth stunted by habits of various kinds. Over all these things victory has been claimed. Brethren have been reconciled to one another; differences which kept sisters apart have been destroyed. Many have testified to victory over novel-reading, dancing, theatre-going, etc. Beyond our ordinary services on Lord's Day, there has been very little or no preaching. While the work has been chiefly confined to the saints of God, purifying, humbling, purging, cleansing, there have been numerous conversions. But these have all taken place during the time of prayer, and prayer usually of a tumultuous sort. One does not readily take in the meaning of simultaneous praying, in a meeting of from 100 to 200 people, full to overflowing of a strong desire to pour out their hearts before the Lord. How could there possibly be time for each to pray separately? After all, what need is there to wait? His ear finds no difficulty in dealing with the simultaneous prayer of a revival meeting.

"We ought not to be disturbed by such happenings. If we could permit ourselves to forget our neighbours and everything else, and remember that we are in the presence of God, we should very soon pass the place where such things could disturb. We appeal for a freedom of the Holy Spirit on our gatherings, and, as one eminent writer has said: 'God save us, lest we civilise the Holy Spirit out of our churches.'

"What the present movement is doing is the creating of a new intensity of love to Jesus, a new sensitiveness to sin, a new desire to have victory in the inner life, a new passion in prayer, and a new expectancy to see God work in power. To all who know anything of the inner spirit of the recent movement, the conviction is given: 'He hath shed forth this which we now see and hear' (Acts ii. 33). This awakening and quickening was so spontaneous and almost unlooked for that we are compelled to acknowledge its Divine origin. It has not passed off and vanished in mere sentiment; nor like a wave of emotion proved itself transient and unreal. It abides. At the moment of writing, it shows no sign of abatement, but rather have we evidence of its deepening and expanding nature. Many who, in the earlier stages of its manifestation, looked coldly, and critically, and suspiciously upon it, have been brought into line with it. For nigh thirty days the Spirit of God has been brooding over us. Come, O Breath, and breathe in this manner upon us now. Amen, O Lord."

A second half-night of prayer was held on January 13, but the spirit and scenes of that meeting baffle description. It was given to some of us to know what Isaiah meant when he said, "The posts of the door moved at the voice of Him that cried."

Some of the choruses of the revival movement were:

He can break every fetter,
He can set you free.

—with variations of "Let Him break every fetter," and "He has broken every fetter"—

Victory for me! through the blood of Christ
my Saviour,
Victory for me! through the precious Blood.

and

> Sinful and black though the past may have been;
> Many the crushing defeats I have seen,
> Yet on Thy promise, O Lord, now I lean,
> Cleansing for me.

The singing of these choruses was the means of bringing many souls from bondage to liberty.

On February 16, 1907, Mr. Kemp wrote: "Among the many remarkable features of the recent spiritual awakening in our midst, none has been more striking than the all-night prayer meeting held on February 16. Beginning at ten o'clock on the Saturday night, it continued until eight o'clock on Lord's Day morning. The only break during the whole night was at two o'clock, when tea was served. Fully two hundred people would be present until that hour, and not fewer than one hundred and fifty remained the whole of the night.

"It is not possible to describe such a meeting; it is necessary to be in it to know it. From the beginning to the close the prayers ascended in one unbroken continuity. At times the prayers rose and fell like the waves of the sea. At half-past three in the morning the scenes were bewildering to behold. It seemed as though everybody in the meeting was praying at once. There was no confusion: nothing unseemly. The passion of prayer had caught the people, and we felt we must pray.

"The Lord's Day following, over a score of souls professed faith in Christ, again proving the faithfulness of our God. Space forbids us entering further into details on this remarkable season of prayer.

"Prayer meetings have been continued nightly, and we look for some brothers and sisters to receive an abiding blessing, which in the days to come will mark them out in a very special way for effective service."

On March 1907 he again writes: "The gracious visitation, reported at some length last month, has deepened as the weeks have gone past. The marked features of the movement are—

"1. A deep conviction of sin, even where the outward life appeared blameless. Nothing has been so remarkable as the searching of heart and the revealing of the 'hidden things.' Many things thought to be right have been seen to be wrong and sinful.

"At one never-to-be-forgotten prayer meeting, as we were approaching midnight, a request for prayer was made by one, that grace might be granted to give us an unconverted sweetheart. No fewer than four similar cases were the subjects of prayer that night, and in each case these unholy attachments were dropped. To very many, 'sin does not appear sin'; but in few things does sin hide its true colors more effectively than in the matter of the 'unequal yoke.' For a child of God, be they man or woman, to allow the affections to be placed upon one who is unconverted, is to commit no light offence against the plain teaching of the Word of God, and must bring with it a whole horde of sorrows. Thank God, many during these weeks of quickening have had shown to them the sinfulness of that line of action, and grace has been given to forsake the evil way.

"Others have been convicted of prayerlessness, indolence, worldliness, temper, bitterness, and so on. Here the 'Doctrine of the doubtful things' applies. A thing which may have been in itself perfectly lawful, has been abandoned because it stood in the way of full surrender and wholehearted consecration.

"2. Another feature is the prolonged intercession sometimes for hours. Our usual seven o'clock prayer meeting, held every Lord's Day morning, has for several weeks commenced at six o'clock and continued until eight o'clock. The 5:45 P.M. prayer meeting starts at 5:30, and such has been the power of God in the meetings that it has been impossible to get to the open air at the usual hour, the Upper Vestry and the Pastor's Vestry and the Library all crowded with praying people. Then again at 9:30 P.M., after the Lord's Day work is over, about sixty have met again for prayer, and continued until after midnight. Here we have learned something of what Wales experienced of prolonged prayer meetings.

"Not only have lengthened meetings been a feature of the work, but the gift of prolonged intercession has been given to several brethren. Losing all consciousness of another's presence, the soul has poured itself out, often audibly, for over an hour. One brother, unknown to any of us, prayed in an agony for the people of his own town for fully an hour and a half. The perspiration was standing on his brow like beads. He was almost too weak to stand when the hour came for closing the chapel, and was literally lifted from his position.

"3. The third marked feature is the new spontaneity and power of the Prayer Meetings. There is no necessity to ask any one to 'improve the time.' The stream of prayer flows on unhindered.

Many who never prayed in public before have found it easy to speak to God in the presence of others. To be in such prayer meetings is the privilege of a lifetime. Before this movement, such meetings were known only by name. They had been features in past revivals, but unknown to the most of us in this day; now they are part of our Christian experience. Prayer at such meetings is not a mere perfunctory exercise, cold and meaningless, but a living vital reality."

Summing up this very remarkable story of revival, Dr. A. C. Dixon, who knew Kemp and his ministry quite intimately, gave this evaluation: "I consider that Mr. Kemp's work in Charlotte Chapel, Edinburgh, to be more lasting and further reaching than the Welsh revival." It may be that some pastor is reading this little book. You ask the question: Could such a thing ever happen in my church? Once again, my answer is that I am sure it could. Do we not believe that "Jesus Christ [is] the same yesterday, and today, and for ever" (Hebrews 13:8)?

Now concerning the mission field. In 1950, my dear friend, Mr. Roy Hession, sent me his prayer letter after a visit to East Africa. This is what he had to say:

Five of us have recently visited East Africa to witness for ourselves the revival that is spreading through Uganda, Kenya, Tanganyika, and Ruanda, and to share in the wonderful blessing that God is pouring out on both Africans and Europeans. Our first "port of call" was to attend a conference of the leaders of revival from all these territories, which was held at Kako in Uganda from April 23rd to 30th. There were present some 100 European missionaries and 600/700 African leaders. That may seem a considerable number, but there would easily have been many times that number, had it not been decided to severely restrict the number of delegates from each area. It was one of the greatest experiences of my life. I had heard a great deal of what God was doing in East Africa, but as I shared in the revival myself, I had just to bow the head and worship and confess that "the half had never been told me."

The first impression that I gained was of the amazing oneness amongst the Christians. Representatives of some 30 tribes, who but a few years ago were continually at one another's throats were seen embracing one another, eating and sleeping together and praising the Lord together, in deepest fellowship. An African King and an African Prime Minister, both of them saved, were as ready to testify to what Jesus had done for them and wave their arms, singing "Tukutenderesa" (the African praise chorus), as were the poorest in the land. Best of all, the grace of God had achieved a wonderful oneness and trust between European and African—no pride or superiority in the one, nor inferiority, resentment and jealousy in the other. They were completely free with one another. Those who know Africa told me that normally there is bitter hatred of the European, and that this is so, even in the professing church, though skilfully hidden under the surface. But here in the revival the love of Jesus shared by all has obliterated the barriers. This fellowship was not created by the European trying to live more and more like the African and be more and more condescending. There have been those who have tried to do this. But when they have done all this, the barriers still remain, and oneness has not been achieved. But when all are willing for self to be broken at the Cross, fellowship is achieved immediately. To think that we must try and change the standard of living to get fellowship is to resort to "works" and to be certain of failure. But whenever men really meet as sinners at the Cross of Christ, fellowship is complete, whatever may be the differing standards of life. And this I saw worked out before my eyes at Kako. For myself, I have never been embraced so much in all my life—and that not merely by Europeans but by Africans, not with a polite handshake, but with real hugs, good and proper. All of us who came from England were overwhelmed with the loving and tumultuous welcome we received.

The second impression I gained was that of the tremendous paean of praise that goes up all the time to the Lord Jesus. The spirit of praise and rejoicing in Him is perhaps one of the most prominent features in the revival. Again and again the addresses would be interrupted by the African praise chorus breaking forth from hearts filled with the vision of the glory of the Lamb. At the close of the service, as the great crowds filed slowly out of the Anglican Church in which the meetings were held, the same hymn and chorus would continually sweep the whole company. And then when they got outside the church, it was only to stand in a great crowd and praise and praise. I was sometimes near to tears as I watched this praise to Jesus for His precious Blood (for that is ever the theme of their song) and I thought how precious it must be to Him. Truly here was the reward of His sufferings.

The praise would reach, however, an even higher level whenever anyone was saved. After the first two days of the conference people began to be saved. There was never any appeal for people to raise their hands or go into an inquiry room. The Holy Spirit Himself would convict a man and he would yield to the Lord Jesus. When he got out of the church, he would begin to testify to one or two around him that he had been saved. The news would quickly spread, and then there would be a scene of rejoicing which it is almost impossible to describe. The first time I saw it, I could hardly believe my eyes. I saw a large crowd of Africans singing praise with more than usual vigour and abandon. As I pushed forward I saw a middle-aged man standing humbly in their midst. One after another Africans were coming up to him and throwing their arms around him and shaking his hand. I learned that he was a deacon of the very church in which we had been meeting. He was a man who had long resisted the call of Jesus but he had just given in and found peace. Suddenly someone would hold up his hand and the singing would be silenced, while he gave his testimony in a few broken sentences. And then the singing of praise would continue with even greater joy and so also would the embracings of the returning sinner. Those of us Europeans who were near embraced him too and sang with the rest. But what a welcome into the kingdom of God for a poor sinner! And this happened for everyone who was saved, or in whom the Lord won a special victory.

Let me tell you of some of the marvels that God did in our midst. It seemed that the Holy Spirit was absolutely free in that atmosphere of praise, and nothing was impossible. The next day was Sunday and at 9 A.M. we had the usual Church of England service, somewhat shortened to enable more time for the messages, of which there were two. The African Rural Dean, who was in charge of both that church and that whole area, read the service. It was a wonderful thing that he had been willing for this great revival conference to be held on his premises at all. He came to all the meetings and seemed to show real interest. The previous day he had uttered one very significant sentence. One of us had been giving him our testimony, and he asked, "Did it take you long to be broken?" We thought that God was working in his heart, but we hardly dared hope for what actually happened that Sunday morning. At the close of the service, clothed in his robes, he came forward to say a few words. Many of the messages had been on the line of Jesus bringing people out of the prison of sin. To our astonishment he said, "I have been one of Satan's jailors all this time, looking after his prisoners. But the prisoners have all escaped. So I have decided to accept the Lord Jesus and be saved too." The Church echoed again and again with praise to God. Some semblance of order was established, while the clergy proceeded down the aisle into the vestry to disrobe. Outside the Africans sang and sang "Tukutenderesa." When he appeared, he was surrounded by the happy rejoicing crowd and hugged and embraced by numberless Africans, and then swept along to his house. While a man is unbroken and unwilling to bend, the Africans are silent and it is quite clear that he is not in fellowship. But the moment he is broken, their love to such an one knows no bounds—even if he is a Rural Dean! That afternoon some of the missionaries visited him and he asked them to join him in prayer. He poured out his heart to God and told Him that that day he was but a newborn babe. This was indeed a notable victory for the Lord Jesus. The news of it is likely to shake deeply the forces of those who oppose the revival.

Later that morning I saw another rejoicing crowd, praising yet another trophy. I learned that it was a notorious backslider who had returned to the Lord. He had been greatly used of God in the early days, but had gone back into sin and for years had been hard and unwilling to yield. But that day he had been broken, and there was yet another to welcome back into the Kingdom.

At dinner time that day in the European marquee, Bill Butler was giving a word of thanks to the various people who had helped with all the work—it was the last day. The African cook was due for our thanks and he was brought in and we gave him a good clap. Bill said to us in English, "He is not yet saved, but if only he served the Lord as faithfully as he has served us, he would make a good brother." Then he translated what he had said into Luganda for him. To which he replied that he decided there and then to accept the Lord Jesus—and that came from a man who had long withstood the Saviour. The tent was filled with praise and from all sides people came forward to embrace him—among them the young African King of Bugufe, who was saved some years ago. What a sight that was, to see a king embracing a cook! What a demonstration of the fact that at His Cross men of all ranks are made one!

In the evening of that day, a friend and myself walked up to the African quarters in the hope that we might be able to take a photo of a crowd of singing Africans. We found a crowd singing all right, and by the waving arms we knew that there must be another victory for Jesus. In their midst was a woman giving her testimony. It was the Rural Dean's wife—she had just bowed her will to the Lord Jesus and been saved. Oh, how we praised the Lamb with our African brothers. And there were others who were saved of whom I have not space to speak, and doubtless yet others, of whose conversion I did not hear. For God was at work everywhere, not only in the meetings but wherever groups of Christians were rejoicing and testifying.

In nearly all these cases, there will be much that the newly saved one will have to put right. The sin has often been flagrant and wilful. But the public manner of their welcome into the Kingdom commits them all the more definitely to make the necessary restitutions. Very little escapes the watchful eyes of the African brethren.

And this sort of thing is happening in an ever increasing area right over East Africa and not only in special conferences such as this one. All the time men and women are being saved, not through great preachers or big campaigns, but through the convincing testimony of a fellowship of saved sinners, who are full of praise to Jesus. Sometimes that fellowship is very small—perhaps in some village. In other places the fellowship is larger, but all the time the witness is being given and the song of praise going up, and all the time sinners are being brought to the Lord Jesus and the fellowship increased. And the wonderful thing is that in no place has this spiritual movement left the Church—in most places it is the Church of England. Had similar blessing come to England, there would have been twenty new sects by now, all of them vying with each other—and that, of course, would have meant the end of the revival.

All this that I have described is, however, only the outwardness of revival. What is the inwardness of it? We can thank God for the outwardness, but a knowledge of that will never bring us revival. If we pray for the same outwardness to be repeated where we are, we shall always be disappointed. Revival does not come by merely praying for it, but by fulfilling the conditions of its inwardness. What then is the inwardness of this spiritual movement which is so deeply affecting the life of East Africa? It is simply that the Christians are being continually broken at the sight of the Lord Jesus on Calvary, in order that the Lord Jesus might be continually just everything to them—their life, their victory, their wisdom, their joy, their strength, their everything. While we are walking in independence and trying in our own strength, He can never be all that to us. Therefore there is the need of continual brokenness. This involves us in real sensitiveness to sin, and in being open to conviction all the time and the willingness to "break," when God puts His finger on anything throughout the day. It means too a new vision of the power of the Blood of Jesus to cleanse and to give us complete victory over all that we are willing to be broken about. I confess this is what God is doing for me and I praise Him for it. If the word "brokenness" is a stumbling block to some, we can call it the willingness to humble ourselves and repent immediately. It means "He must increase, but I must decrease." This, as I understand it, is the true inwardness of the revival here and indeed of revival anywhere and at any time. This was the whole purpose of the conference I have described. The purpose of the conference was not primarily evangelistic at all. It was simply that the leaders of the revival might be more deeply broken, and that the Lord Jesus might be more completely their All. And this the Lord did for us, both Europeans and Africans, in a very wonderful way. Sin was revealed in our lives to which we had for a long time been turning a blind eye, attitudes of self which had separated us from our brethren were brought to the Cross and confessed and many prisons in which God's people had been shut up were opened and prisoners went out free. And as this was happening, those who had never been saved, were convicted and broken and saved too. If I may say so, the remarkable cases of conversion which I have recorded here were but the by-product of Christians being broken before the Lord. Not that there is no direct witness to the unconverted in this revival—there is plenty—but it is personal witness uttered by men who are continually humbling themselves before God for the smallest sin and proving continually the power of the precious Blood of Christ to cleanse.

What a difference it would make on the mission fields of the world if the overseas churches were to be visited by a similar outpouring of the Holy Spirit! What solutions there would be to the problems of field operations and how easy would be the task of home councils! Is it not time that missionary statesmen, as well as pastors of churches in the homeland, give more attention to the crying need for prayer, faith, and revival, than to all the organizing and high promotional methods of the modern day?

So whether it be in the personal life, in the church life, or on the mission field, we need revival, we need revival urgently, we need revival desperately. Oh, that our heart-cry might be:

> Let it come, O Lord, we pray Thee;
> Let the showers of blessing fall.
> We are waiting and "expecting,"
> O revive the hearts of all.

James L. Black